Pub Walks & Cycle Rides

The Cotswolds

Walk routes researched and written by David Hancock, Dennis Kelsall, Christopher Knowles
Cycle routes researched and written by Dennis Kelsall
Series managing editor: David Hancock

Produced by AA Publishing
© Automobile Association Developments Ltd 2005
First published 2005

Published by AA Publishing (a trading name of Automobile Association Developments Limited, whose registered office is Southwood East, Apollo Rise, Farnborough, Hampshire, GU14 0JW; registered number 1878835).

A02013

ISBN-10: 0-7495-4448-1
ISBN-13: 978-0-7495-4448-5

A CIP catalogue record for this book is available from the British Library.

The contents of this book are believed correct at the time of printing. Nevertheless, the publishers cannot be held responsible for any errors or omissions or for changes in the details given in this book or for the consequences of any reliance on the information it provides. We have tried to ensure accuracy in this book, but things do change and we would be grateful if readers would advise us of any inaccuracies they may encounter. This does not affect your statutory rights.

We have taken all reasonable steps to ensure that these walks and cycle rides are safe and achievable by people with a realistic level of fitness. However, all outdoor activities involve a degree of risk and the publishers accept no responsibility for any injuries caused to readers whilst following these walks and cycle rides. For advice on walking and cycling in safety, see pages 12 to 15.

Visit AA Publishing's website www.theAA.com/bookshop

Page layouts by pentacorbig, High Wycombe
Colour reproduction by Keene Group, Andover
Printed in Spain by Graficas Estella

AA

Pub Walks & Cycle Rides

The Cotswolds

Locator map

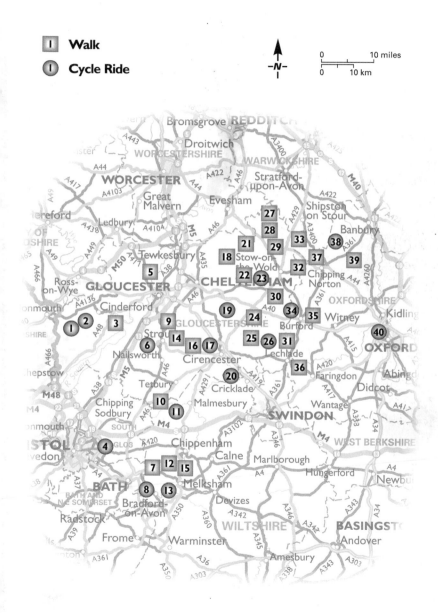

I **Walk**

① **Cycle Ride**

0 ——— 10 miles
0 ——— 10 km

-N-

Contents

Picture on page 4: View from Painswick Beacon in northwest Gloucestershire

Contents

The Cotswolds

The area known as the Cotswolds takes in Gloucestershire, Wiltshire, Oxfordshire, northeast Somerset and even extends into Worcestershire and Warwickshire, although most of the area falls within the boundaries of just one county, Gloucestershire. The region is known for its distinctive honey-coloured Cotswold stone cottages and quintessential, pretty, English villages such as Lacock (with Lacock Abbey), Bibury, Chipping Campden and Burford (which is often referred to as the gateway to the Cotswolds). It's a region full of potential for those who love the great outdoors. For walkers there's the Cotswold Way National Trail (all 101 miles/163km of it), for cyclists there are miles of easy-to-navigate dedicated cycle paths (formerly working railway lines), for bird watchers there are several bird reserves, and for watersports fans there are lakes for sailing, kayaking, jetskiing or fishing.

There are plenty of interesting places to visit after your walk or cycle, or if you cut short your trip in the event of bad weather. Bird lovers will appreciate the Wildfowl and Wetland Centre at Slimbridge, and gardeners will want to stop off at Kiftsgate

Court or Hidcote Manor Garden. There's also the elegant Georgian architecture of Bath, historic Malmesbury Abbey, Sudeley Castle just outside Winchcombe, or Kelmscott Manor, William Morris's country home. If you've sampled some of the local ale at the pub on route, you may appreciate a tour of the Cotswolds' own brewery, Hook Norton. If history is more your thing, choose the route which takes in the Roman villa at Chedworth or the route past the prehistoric megalithic monuments, the Rollright Stones, which are near Chipping Norton. There are also the twin churches of Eastleach Turville and Eastleach Martin, or the interestingly named villages Guiting Power, or Upper and Lower Slaughter.

For a cycle with the minimum of climbing, choose the routes which follow the old Severn & Wye Railway or the former Avon Valley Railway. For greenery, head to the far fringes of the Cotswolds, the Forest of Dean, and for a waterside route, walk along the River Severn or the River Thames, or cycle around the manmade lakes of the Cotswold Water Park.

You are spoilt for choice in terms of charming pubs, many of which serve excellent food. Pubs include a converted 16th-century corn mill with two working water wheels, historic centuries-old pubs, pubs with play areas and beautiful gardens, and even one with boules pitches and a skittles alley. Many pubs, especially on the Cotswold Way, have thoughtfully provided facilities specifically for walkers and cyclists, such as a drying room for wet gear.

The River Coln in Gloucestershire

Using this book

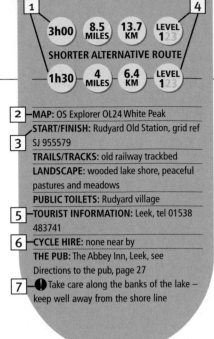

Each walk and cycle ride has a coloured panel giving essential information for the walker and cyclist, including the distance, terrain, nature of the paths, and where to park your car.

1 **MINIMUM TIME:** The time stated for completing each route is the estimated minimum time that a reasonably fit family group of walkers or cyclists would take to complete the circuit. This does not allow for rest or refreshment stops.

2 **MAPS:** Each route is shown on a detailed map. However, some detail is lost because of the restrictions imposed by scale, so for this reason, we recommend that you use the maps in conjunction with a more detailed Ordnance Survey map. The relevant Ordnance Survey Explorer map appropriate for each walk or cycle is listed.

3 **START/FINISH:** Here we indicate the start location and parking area. There is a six-figure grid reference prefixed by two letters showing which 100km square of the National Grid it refers to. You'll find more information on grid references on most Ordnance Survey maps.

4 **LEVEL OF DIFFICULTY:** The walks and cycle rides have been graded simply (1 to 3) to give an indication of their relative difficulty. Easier routes, such as those with little total ascent, on easy footpaths or level trails, or those covering shorter distances are graded 1. The hardest routes, either

because they include a lot of ascent, greater distances, or are in hilly, more demanding terrains, are graded 3.

5 **TOURIST INFORMATION:** The nearest tourist information office and contact number is given for further local information, in particular opening details for the attractions listed in the 'Where to go from here' section.

6 **CYCLE HIRE:** We list, within reason, the nearest cycle hire shop/centre.

7 ● Here we highlight any potential difficulties or dangers along the route. At a glance you will know if the walk is steep or crosses difficult terrain, or if a cycle route is hilly, encounters a main road, or whether a mountain bike is essential for the off-road trails. If a particular route is suitable for older, fitter children we say so here.

1
3h00 — **8.5 MILES** — **13.7 KM** — **LEVEL 1**23 — **4**
SHORTER ALTERNATIVE ROUTE
1h30 — **4 MILES** — **6.4 KM** — **LEVEL 1**23

2 **MAP:** OS Explorer OL24 White Peak
3 **START/FINISH:** Rudyard Old Station, grid ref SJ 955579
TRAILS/TRACKS: old railway trackbed
LANDSCAPE: wooded lake shore, peaceful pastures and meadows
PUBLIC TOILETS: Rudyard village
5 **TOURIST INFORMATION:** Leek, tel 01538 483741
6 **CYCLE HIRE:** none near by
THE PUB: The Abbey Inn, Leek, see Directions to the pub, page 27
7 ● Take care along the banks of the lake – keep well away from the shore line

About the pub

Generally, all the pubs featured are on the walk or cycle route. Some are close to the start/finish point, others are at the midway point, and occasionally, the recommended pub is a short drive from the start/finish point. We have included a cross-section of pubs, from homely village locals and isolated rural gems to traditional inns and upmarket country pubs which specialise in food. What they all have in common is that they serve food and welcome children.

The description of the pub is intended to convey its history and character and in the 'food' section we list a selection of dishes, which indicate the style of food available. Under 'family facilities', we say if the pub offers a children's menu or smaller portions of adult dishes, and whether the pub has a family room, highchairs, baby-changing facilities, or toys. There is detail on the garden, terrace, and any play area.

DIRECTIONS: If the pub is very close to the start point we state see Getting to the Start. If the pub is on the route the relevant direction/map location number is given, in addition to general directions. In some cases the pub is a short drive away from the finish point, so we give detailed directions to the pub from the end of the route.

PARKING: The number of parking spaces is given. All but a few of the walks and rides start away from the pub. If the pub car park is the parking/start point, then we have been given permission by the landlord to print the fact. You should always let the landlord or a member of staff know that you are using the car park before setting off.

OPEN: If the pub is open all week we state 'daily' and if it's open throughout the day we say 'all day', otherwise we just give the days/sessions the pub is closed.

FOOD: If the pub serves food all week we state 'daily' and if food is served throughout the day we say 'all day', otherwise we just give the days/sessions when food is not served.

BREWERY/COMPANY: This is the name of the brewery to which the pub is tied or the pub company that owns it. 'Free house' means that the pub is independently owned and run.

REAL ALE: We list the regular real ales available on handpump. 'Guest beers' indicates that the pub rotates beers from a number of microbreweries.

DOGS: We say if dogs are allowed in pubs on walk routes and detail any restrictions.

ROOMS: We list the number of bedrooms and how many are en suite. For prices please call the pub.

Please note that pubs change hands frequently and new chefs are employed, so menu details and facilities may change at short notice. Not all the pubs featured in this guide are listed in the *AA Pub Guide*. For information on those that are, including AA-rated accommodation, and for a comprehensive selection of pubs across Britain, please refer to the *AA Pub Guide* or see the AA's website www.theAA.com

Alternative refreshment stops
At a glance you will see if there are other pubs or cafés along the route. If there are no other places on the route, we list the nearest village or town where you can find somewhere else to eat and drink.

☛ Where to go from here
Many of the routes are short and may only take a few hours. You may wish to explore the surrounding area after lunch or before tackling the route, so we have selected a few attractions with children in mind.

Walking and cycling in safety

WALKING

All the walks are suitable for families, but less experienced family groups, especially those with younger children, should try the shorter or easier walks first. Route finding is usually straightforward, but the maps are for guidance only and we recommend that you always take the suggested Ordnance Survey map with you.

Risks

Although each walk has been researched with a view to minimising any risks, no walk in the countryside can be considered to be completely free from risk. Walking in the outdoors will always require a degree of common sense and judgement to ensure that it is as safe as possible, especially for young children.

- Be particularly careful on cliff paths and in upland terrain, where the consequences of a slip can be serious.
- Remember to check tidal conditions before walking on the seashore.
- Some sections of route are by, or cross, busy roads. Remember traffic is a danger even on minor country lanes.
- Be careful around farmyard machinery and livestock.
- Be aware of the consequences of changes in the weather and check the forecast before you set out. Ensure the whole family is properly equipped, wearing warm clothing and a good pair of boots or sturdy walking shoes. Take waterproof clothing with you and carry spare clothing and a torch if you are walking in the winter months. Remember the weather can change quickly at any time of the year, and in moorland and heathland areas, mist and fog can make route finding much harder. In summer, take account of the heat and sun by wearing a hat and carrying enough water.

- On walks away from centres of population you should carry a whistle and survival bag. If you do have an accident requiring emergency services, make a note of your position as accurately as possible and dial 999.

CYCLING

Cycling is a fun activity which children love, and teaching your child to ride a bike, and going on family cycling trips, are rewarding experiences. Not only is cycling a great way to travel, but as a regular form of exercise it can make an invaluable contribution to a child's health and fitness, and increase their confidence and sense of independence.

The growth of motor traffic has made Britain's roads increasingly dangerous and unattractive to cyclists. Cycling with children is an added responsibility and, as with everything, there is a risk when taking them out for a day's cycling. However, in recent years many measures have been taken to address this, including the on-going development of the National Cycle Network (8,000 miles utilising quiet lanes and traffic-free paths) and local designated off-road routes for families, such as converted railway lines, canal towpaths and forest tracks.

In devising the cycle rides in this guide, every effort has been made to use these designated cycle paths, or to link

them with quiet country lanes and waymarked byways and bridleways. Unavoidably, in a few cases, some relatively busy B-roads have been used to link the quieter, more attractive routes.

Rules of the road

- Ride in single file on narrow and busy roads.
- Be alert, look and listen for traffic, especially on narrow lanes and blind bends and be extra careful when descending steep hills, as loose gravel can lead to an accident.
- In wet weather make sure you keep a good distance between you and other riders.
- Make sure you indicate your intentions clearly.
- Brush up on *The Highway Code* before venturing out on to the road.

Off-road safety code of conduct

- Only ride where you know it is legal to do so. It is forbidden to cycle on public footpaths, marked in yellow. The only 'rights of way' open to cyclists are bridleways (blue markers) and unsurfaced tracks, known as byways, which are open to all traffic and waymarked in red.
  - Canal towpaths: you need a permit to cycle on some stretches of towpath (www.waterscape.com). Remember that access paths can be steep and slippery and always get off and push your bike under low bridges and by locks.

13

- Always yield to walkers and horses, giving adequate warning of your approach.
- Don't expect to cycle at high speeds.
- Keep to the main trail to avoid any unnecessary erosion to the area beside the trail and to prevent skidding, especially if it is wet.
- Remember the Country Code.

Cycling with children

Children can use a child seat from the age of eight months, or from the time they can hold themselves upright. There are a number of child seats available which fit on the front or rear of a bike and towable two-seat trailers are worth investigating. 'Trailer bicycles', suitable for five- to ten-year-olds, can be attached to the rear of an adult's bike, so that the adult has control, allowing the child to pedal if he/she wishes. Family cycling can be made easier by using a tandem, as it can carry a child seat and tow trailers. 'Kiddy-cranks' for shorter legs can be fitted to the rear seat tube, enabling either parent to take their child out cycling. With older children it is better to purchase the right size bike rather than one that is too big, as an oversized bike will be difficult to control, and potentially dangerous.

Preparing your bicycle

A basic routine includes checking the wheels for broken spokes or excess play in the bearings, and checking the tyres for punctures, undue wear and the correct tyre pressures. Ensure that the brake blocks are firmly in place and not worn, and that cables are not frayed or too slack. Lubricate hubs, pedals, gear mechanisms and cables. Make sure you have a pump, a bell, a rear rack to carry panniers and, if cycling at night, a set of working lights.

Preparing yourself

Equipping the family with cycling clothing need not be an expensive exercise. Comfort is the key when considering what to wear. Essential items for well-being on a bike are padded cycling shorts, warm stretch leggings (avoid tight-fitting and seamed trousers like jeans or baggy tracksuit trousers that may become caught in the chain), stiff-soled training shoes, and a wind and waterproof jacket. Fingerless gloves will add to your comfort.

A cycling helmet provides essential protection if you fall off your bike, so they are particularly recommended for young children learning to cycle.

Wrap your child up with several layers in colder weather. Make sure you and those with you are easily visible by car drivers and other road users, by wearing light-coloured or luminous clothing in daylight and reflective strips or sashes in failing light and when it is dark.

What to take with you

Invest in a pair of medium-sized panniers (rucksacks are unwieldy and can affect balance) to carry the necessary gear for you and your family for the day. Take extra clothes with you, the amount depending on the season, and always pack a light wind/waterproof jacket. Carry a basic tool kit (tyre levers, adjustable spanner, a small screwdriver, puncture repair kit, a set of Allen keys) and practical spares, such as an inner tube, a universal brake/gear cable, and a selection of nuts and bolts. Also, always take a pump and a strong lock.

Cycling, especially in hilly terrain and off-road, saps energy, so take enough food and drink for your outing. Always carry plenty of water, especially in hot and humid weather conditions. Consume high-energy snacks like cereal bars, cake or fruits, eating little and often to combat feeling weak and tired. Remember that children get thirsty (and hungry) much more quickly than adults so always have food and diluted juices available for them.

And finally, the most important advice of all–enjoy yourselves!

USEFUL CYCLING WEBSITES

NATIONAL CYCLE NETWORK
A comprehensive network of safe and attractive cycle routes throughout the UK.
It is co-ordinated by the route construction charity Sustrans with the support of more than 450 local authorities and partners across Britain. For maps, leaflets and more information on the designated off-road cycle trails across the country contact
www.sustrans.org.uk
www.nationalcyclenetwork.org.uk

LONDON CYCLING CAMPAIGN
Pressure group that lobbies MPs, organises campaigns and petitions in order to improve cycling conditions in the capital. It provides maps, leaflets and information on cycle routes across London.
www.lcc.org.uk

BRITISH WATERWAYS
For information on towpath cycling, visit
www.waterscape.com

FORESTRY COMMISSION
For information on cycling in Forestry Commission woodland see
www.forestry.gov.uk/recreation

CYCLISTS TOURING CLUB
The largest cycling club in Britain, provides information on cycle touring, and legal and technical matters
www.ctc.org.uk

Coleford to Parkend and Cannop Ponds

Follow a 19th-century railway to discover man-made pools, now a haven for wildlife.

Iron ore mining

Long before the Romans arrived, iron ore was mined in the forest and smelted in crude hearths using charcoal derived from the abundant supplies of timber. Methods changed little until the end of the 18th century, when the gathering pace of the Industrial Revolution demanded metals with greater hardness and flexibility than wrought- and cast-iron could offer. David and Robert Mushet, a father and son from Coleford, were among the pioneers of steel production: their expertise helped pave the way for a new age. Born in 1772, David established a small foundry at Cinderhill, later building a much larger ironworks at Dark Hill, which his son took over in 1847. Robert experimented to improve Bessemer's steel process, adding carbon and manganese to reduce brittleness and imperfections in castings. His discovery found an immediate application in the railways, whose early tracks were prone to rapid failure as they cracked under the rumbling wheels. The first steel rails were used at Derby in 1857, where they instantly proved their worth, allowing heavier loads and faster speeds than could ever have been achieved along a cast-iron track. Robert went on to develop the first tungsten steel, an alloy hard enough to be used as a cutting tool for machining metal components.

the ride

1 Leave the car park, crossing the B4228, a sometimes busy road, to reach the beginning of the **cycle path** opposite. The way is signed to Parkend and begins with a gentle climb beside the town's golf

Reeds fringing the ponds at Cannop Wharf Nature Reserve

2h30	**11** MILES	**17.7** KM	LEVEL 1**2**3

MAP: OS Explorer OL14 Wye Valley & Forest of Dean

START/FINISH: Coleford. Car park beside B4228; grid ref: SO 577104

TRAILS/TRACKS: firm cycle trails

LANDSCAPE: forest and woodland

PUBLIC TOILETS: near car park

TOURIST INFORMATION: Coleford, tel 01594 812388

CYCLE HIRE: Pedalabikeaway Cycle Centre, New Road, Forest of Dean, tel 01594 860065; www.pedalabikeaway.com

THE PUB: The Woodman, Parkend

 A long outward descent and steady climb back, 4 road crossings (in each direction), overhanging twigs; route shared with pedestrians

Getting to the start

Coleford lies at the edge of the Forest of Dean, some 20 miles (32.2km) south west of Gloucester. The ride begins from a car park on the right beside the B4228, as it leaves the town heading south.

Why do this cycle ride?

This off-road route from Coleford to the heart of the Forest of Dean, follows a disused branch of the Severn and Wye Railway and Canal Company's line. The ride ends at the popular Cannop Wharf Nature Reserve and picnic spot beside Cannop Ponds, created at the beginning of the 19th century to store water for iron works further down the valley.

Researched and written by: Dennis Kelsall

course. After crossing a second road, again take care, the track shortly enters the fringe of the forest, passing the ruins of the former **Dark Hill Iron Works**. Plant-bearded walls are all that remain of the furnaces, sheds and stores, rising in steps up the valley side; they look more like abandoned cultivated terraces than a one-time industrial factory. Not far beyond there, the track twists around to cross a third road.

2 The way continues in a long and winding descent along the valley, later passing the disused **Point Quarry**, slowly being colonised by birch and gorse. In the cutting just beyond, the fine sandstone that was worked is exposed beside the cycle track. There is a **working stone yard** at Cannop, at the foot of the lakes on the opposite side of the valley to the track,

Ducks at Cannop Ponds

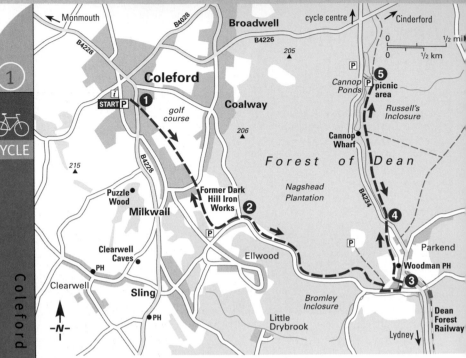

where the same warm-coloured sandstone is still cut and dressed. Be careful to control your speed as you continue, since a little way after the quarry, and without advance warning, the route drops across an access drive. Keep ahead at a second junction, the way now signed to **Cannop Wharf**, the trail skirting the perimeter of a timber works. It then briefly joins the road at Parkend, sharing the pavement as far as **Hughes Terrace**, off on the left.

3 The trail leads past a row of cottages to end at a turning circle, from the far left of which the cycleway continues. The track passes the site of **Coleford Railway Junction**, with marshalling yards where coal wagons were sorted as they passed up and down the valley to and from the different pits. A little further on is another road crossing, this time the B4234.

4 The ongoing track climbs gently away through the forest, before long reaching a junction at **Cannop Wharf**. Footpaths on the left allow you to explore the nature reserve, home to reed bunting, wood warblers and marsh tits. However, to do this you will have to leave your bikes so remember to bring a lock. Alternatively, you can carry on a little further along the main track beside **Cannop Ponds** to find a picnic area at the top end.

5 Although a return to Coleford along Speech House Road, the B4226, a little way to the north, is possible, there is no off-road route other than the way you have come. Unfortunately it involves more climbing than descent, but there are refreshments at The Woodman at **Parkend**. Just follow the road left as you emerge from Hughes Terrace.

The Woodman

Beyond the plain whitewashed exterior of The Woodman, formerly a coaching inn and now a traditional village pub, you'll find a roomy and relaxing stripped-stone bar, with open fires, a comfortable mix of pub furnishings, beamed ceilings, and walls decorated with old implements once used by the forest woodsmen. Expect a friendly welcome from the hands-on landlord and staff, well-kept real ale and good range of home-cooked pub food. Summer seating in the rear garden and on the front terrace overlooking the village green.

about the pub

The Woodman
Parkend, Lydney
Gloucestershire GL15 4JF
Tel: 01594 563273
www.woodman-parkend.co.uk

DIRECTIONS: opposite the cricket ground in the village

PARKING: 30

OPEN: daily

FOOD: daily

BREWERY/COMPANY: Enterprise Inns

REAL ALE: Wadworth 6X, Greene King Old Speckled Hen, Fuller's London Pride

ROOMS: 5 bedrooms

Food
The wide-ranging menu caters for all tastes, from ploughman's lunches and bacon sandwiches on the snack menu to grilled sardines, fishcakes with chilli dip, rabbit en croute, beef and ale pie, rack of ribs with barbeque sauce, and game casserole on the main menu. Sunday roast lunches.

Family facilities
Families are welcome in the pub and young children can choose from their own menu.

Alternative refreshment stops
Choice of pubs in Coleford and The Speech House (see Route 2) is only a short drive away; picnic areas in forest.

☞ Where to go from here
Visit Clearwell Caves Ancient Iron Mines and explore nine natural caverns that have been mined since earliest times for paint pigment and iron ore (www.clearwellcaves.com). At the Forest of Dean Railway in Lydney (www.deanforestrailway.co.uk), families can see steam locomotives and old railway equipment, and travel on the steam railway.

Forest of Dean family trail

Meander through an ancient forest, where Nelson ordered the planting of oaks to build British man-of-war ships.

Forest of Dean

In 1938, the Forest of Dean was designated England's first National Forest Park, and notwithstanding its wonderfully peaceful and unspoiled setting, it is a working forest from which hundreds of tonnes of timber are harvested annually. It has also been a source of coal, and almost everywhere within the forest bears some evidence of its industrial past.

The criss-crossing leisure paths often follow the network of rail- and tramways that serviced the collieries, while heaps of spoil mark the site of the deeper workings. Contrasting with the luxuriant growth of the surrounding forest, many of these are still uncolonised except by the hardiest plants, the barren shales providing little nutrient despite the weathering of 50 years or more since they were last worked. At one time there were more than ten large pits, with countless small drift and bell mines being worked from antiquity. Although large-scale mining came to an end in 1965, anyone born within the Hundred of St Briavels, over the age of 21, and who has worked for a year and a day in a mine is still entitled to work a 'gale' in the forest as a Free Miner. The privilege was bestowed by Edward I, after forest miners helped ensure his victory at the Siege of Berwick by undermining the castle walls.

A pretty bluebell wood in the Forest of Dean

the ride

1 The cycleway is signed from beside the hire shop along a track that drops steeply to the B4234. Opposite, there is a brief but steep pull to a junction. Go left and left again to join the cycleway in the direction of Drybrook Road Station, gently rising along the course of a disused mineral railway. At **Whitegates Junction**, fork left, dropping with the main track to another obvious junction at which, turn sharp right. Where the track then divides, bear right, still following signs for Drybrook Road Station. Keep going, passing beneath a graceful horseshoe-shaped bridge before shortly encountering a tarmac track at **Drybrook Road Station**.

2 Cross and carry on along the cycleway, which is now signed to **Dilke Bridge**, the earlier gradual climb rewarded with a gentle descent. Soon, the forest clears and the scars of former coal workings become evident. Hazard signs warn of a crossing track hidden in a dip, the way continuing beyond the former **Foxes Bridge Colliery**. After a moderate descent (watch for a bend at the bottom), carry on past a junction for Cinderford Linear Park and then the

outbuildings of Dilke Hospital to arrive at **Dilke Bridge**.

3 Beyond, more hazard signs announce a junction where a broad track joins from the left signed to Cannop Wharf. After a traffic barrier and the former **Lightmore Colliery**, a gate forces you to dismount. There follows a short but stiff pull, the track then bending sharply left before dropping once more past a couple of warned junctions, at the second of which, Spruce Ride to the right, offers a short-cut back via **Speech House**.

4 Otherwise, carry on to Central Bridge across **Blackpool Brook**, later reaching a crossing of tracks where Cannop Wharf and the Cycle Centre are signed right. After a turning to New Fancy picnic site, the track swings to a gate, a little distance beyond which is a road crossing.

5 Through another gate at Burnt Log, the track winds down to a fork. Keep ahead, before long coming to a notice warning of a steep descent. The main track drops through a sharply twisting 'S' bend, passing a massive ancient oak, the last survivor of The Three Brothers, where men from the nearby

---

2h30	9.25 MILES	14.9 KM	LEVEL 123

MAP: OS Explorer OL14 Wye Valley & Forest of Dean

START/FINISH: Car park, Pedalabikeaway Cycle Centre; grid ref: SO 606124

TRAILS/TRACKS: good surfaced cycle trails

LANDSCAPE: forest and woodland

PUBLIC TOILETS: at Pedalabikeaway Cycle Centre (also showers & changing rooms)

TOURIST INFORMATION: Coleford, tel 01594 812388

CYCLE HIRE: Pedalabikeaway Cycle Centre, New Road, Forest of Dean, tel 01594 860065; www.pedalabikeaway.com

THE PUB: The Speech House Hotel, Coleford

🛈 Gradual climbs and descents, one steep descent, 4 road crossings, overhanging twigs; route shared with pedestrians

Getting to the start

Pedalabikeaway Cycle Centre is in the Forest of Dean, 3 miles (4.8km) north east of Coleford beside the B4234.

Why do this cycle ride?

Decreed a royal hunting forest by King Canute in 1016, the Forest of Dean is steeped in a long history. Iron was smelted here before the Romans arrived and they valued not only the timber but also the abundant mineral reserves here – good-quality building stone, coal and iron ore – and began industries that continue to the present day.

Researched and written by: Dennis Kelsall

collieries gathered on a Sunday morning for their union meetings. Beyond, the descent continues more easily, eventually ending at a T-junction beside **Cannop Wharf**.

6 The **Cycle Centre** is signed to the right beside a couple of **artificial lakes**, at the top of which a car park and picnic area are laid out. As the metalled drive bends towards a road, branch off right to a

crossing point over the B4226. Speech House lies 0.5 mile (800m) to the right, although you may wish to return later in the car, whilst the way back is with the continuing track. Fork left when you reach a split, gently losing height to a second junction. There go left again, dropping steeply to the road. Go slowly for there is a sharp bend at the bottom. The **car park** is then at the top of the rise opposite.

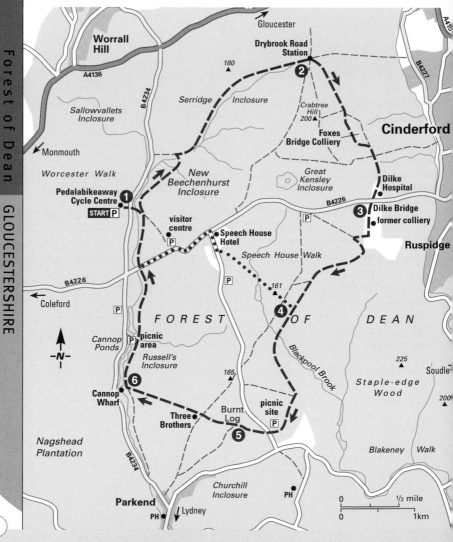

The Speech House Hotel

In the heart of Forest of Dean, close to miles of woodland trails, The Speech House was built in 1676 as a hunting lodge for Charles II. Later it became the administrative centre of the forest. The largest room was the Verderer's Court where people went to talk or make a speech, hence the name of what is now a substantial hotel. The Verderer's Court still meets four times a year in what is Britain's oldest functioning courtroom and it retains much of its original decoration. Despite its hotel status, there's a good bar area with real ale on tap, notably a beer from Whittington's brewery in nearby Newent, a traditional bar menu, and a warm welcome for walkers and cyclists. To the rear there are extensive lawns and gardens for all to use.

Food

Hearty snacks in the bar include sandwiches (beef and horseradish) served with chips, various salads and traditional dishes such as ham, egg and chips, sausages and mash, and battered cod and chips. Separate restaurant menu and Sunday roast lunches.

Family facilities

Children are genuinely welcomed (extra beds and cots are provided if staying), and the welcome extends into the bar and dining area. Here there are high chairs and young children have a standard menu to choose from.

Alternative refreshment stops

Café at the Cycle Hire Centre at start and picnic areas in the forest.

☞ Where to go from here

Learn about the history and culture of the Forest of Dean at the Dean Heritage Centre at Soudley (www.deanheritagemuseum.com) where attractions include a forester's cottage, agricultural displays, blacksmiths and craft units. At Puzzlewood in Coleford, an unusual maze takes you through 24.5ha (14 acres) of pathways, deep ravines and passageways within pre-Roman open-cast iron ore mines.

about the pub

The Speech House Hotel
Coleford, Forest of Dean
Gloucestershire GL16 7EL
Tel: 01594 822607
www.thespeechhouse.co.uk

DIRECTIONS: beside the B4226 between Coleford and Cinderford, at the junction with a minor road for Lydney

PARKING: 60

OPEN: daily; all day

FOOD: daily

BREWERY/COMPANY: free house

REAL ALE: Bass, Whittington's Cat Whiskers

ROOMS: 37 en suite

The Severn Bore at Arlingham

A long but fairly level walk along the river where Britain's regular tidal wave rushes in.

Bore formula

The River Severn is at its most impressive around Arlingham – in its lower reaches before opening up to the Bristol Channel. Here Gloucestershire juts out into the river to form a large promontory, forcing the river into a huge sweeping loop, widening to well over half a mile (800m) at certain points. To the west it is overlooked by the Forest of Dean ridge, to the east by the Cotswold escarpment.

Shallow and placid though it might appear here, the River Severn has a capricious nature. The area has been devastated by floods in the past. The Severn Bore, for which the river is justly famous, is a tidal wave formed a little way downstream, where the river narrows at Sharpness. The fundamental cause behind the bore is the combination of a large volume of tidal water, funnelled into a quickly narrowing channel, hastening on to rock rising from the riverbed. A wave is created, which is then free to roll on to the Severn's middle reaches.

Flooding, however, is rarely a problem here now, because the flood control measures you see as you walk have succeeded in containing the river. It does, though, continue to create havoc every winter further upstream. Significant sea tides at the river's wide mouth make the Severn Bore such a spectacle. In fortnightly cycles over the course of each month the tides reach their highest and lowest points.

Near the Severn Bridge the second highest rise and fall of tide in the world has been recorded (the first is in Canada, on the Petitcodiac River). Once a month, for a few days, the spring tides occur, reaching a height of 31ft (9.4m) at Sharpness. Whenever the tides reach 26ft (8m) or more, a bore will be unleashed.

the walk

1 Leave the crossroads at the centre of Arlingham along Church Lane, opposite the Red Lion. After 0.25 mile (400m), where the lane turns sharply right, keep ahead through a gate along a waymarked track that leads to the river. Climb onto the flood bank.

2 Turn left over a stile and, passing from field to field, follow the river downstream. Keep on for a mile (1.6km), eventually crossing a stile into the corner of a field that rises ahead to a wood on top of **Hock Cliff**.

Arlingham sits on a spur of land that is bounded by the Severn

WALK

Arlingham

GLOUCESTERSHIRE

3 At that point, turn from the river beside the hedge. Where it doglegs half-way along, pass over a stiled bridge to continue in the adjacent field. Emerging at the corner onto a track, go left towards a **barn** but before reaching it, look for a stile on the right. A hedged path leads away to meet a lane.

4 Cross to a drive opposite signed to **Colthill**. After winding right in front of one cottage the track ends before another. Slip through an opening on the left and walk at the garden edge to a stile in the corner. Keep ahead beside the field boundary, passing into the next field to climb past a couple of **houses**. Just beyond the second house, turn over a stile on the right into a small field. Bear left to a second stile half-way along the opposite hedge to reach a lane.

5 Follow it left through **Overton** for just over 0.5 mile (800m), leaving over a stile beside a gate on the left as the lane bends sharply right before a long house. Once more by the Severn, head downstream, shortly crossing a stile into a

3h15 — **7.5 MILES** — **12.1 KM** — **LEVEL 1 2 3**

MAP: OS Explorer OL 14 Wye Valley & Forest of Dean

START/FINISH: Arlingham village; grid ref: ST 708109

PATHS: tracks, fields and lanes, 26 stiles

LANDSCAPE: river, meadows and distant hills

PUBLIC TOILETS: none on route

TOURIST INFORMATION: Gloucester, tel 01452 396572

THE PUB: The Red Lion, Arlingham

🛈 Although quite long the walk is suitable for all ages; no real hazards

Getting to the start

Arlingham occupies a promontory of the River Severn, 9 miles (14.5km) south west of Gloucester and not far from Junction 13 on the M5. You will find roadside parking in the centre of the village near The Red Lion.

Researched and written by: Dennis Kelsall, Christopher Knowles

strip of scrubby woodland. At the far side, the path winds through tall reeds before crossing a stile into a crop field. Go right along the edge, turning the corner to find a **plank bridge** and stile about 15yds (14m) along. Carry on ahead, rejoining the riverbank to progress through successive fields.

6 Later climbing onto a flood dyke, the way continues ahead, eventually rounding a sharp bend in the river and then passing **Newnham** on the opposite bank. Keep going until you reach The Old Passage Inn.

7 Turn in beside it, following the lane for 0.75 mile (1.2km) across the flood plain back to **Arlingham**.

what to look for

Hock Cliff, composed of clay and limestone, is well-known for its fossils, including the so-called Devil's toenails, ammonites, belemnites and many others. Towards the walk's end, approaching the Old Passage Inn, you will see Newnham across the river. Tradition has it that the Romans crossed the river here by elephant to attack fugitive Britons.

The Red Lion

Summer flower baskets add a splash of colour at this old stone pub on a crossroads in the heart of the village. Expect a cosy interior and a friendly atmosphere, typical of a well-managed community local, although the pub is fast making something of a name for itself locally for the quality of its food. Imaginative, restaurant-style menus draw discerning diners to the door but there remains a warm welcome for walkers and few will be disappointed with the lighter meals available at lunchtime, or the decent range of ales on tap. On warmer days you can sit outside in the small and sheltered patio garden or at pavement tables overlooking the village.

about the pub

The Red Lion
Arlingham, Gloucester
Gloucestershire GL2 7JN
Tel: 01452 740700

DIRECTIONS: see Getting to the Start

PARKING: 8 (+ roadside parking)

OPEN: all day Saturday & Sunday; closed all Monday (except Bank Holidays) and Tuesday lunchtime

FOOD: no food Sunday evening

BREWERY/COMPANY: Enterprise Inns

REAL ALE: Fuller's London Pride, Caledonian Deuchars IPA, guest beers

DOGS: allowed in the bar area only

ROOMS: 3 en suite

Food

From the 'lite bite' menu you could choose a ploughman's lunch, pasta carbonara, beer-battered haddock and chips, pork and chive sausages with mash and onion gravy or Thai-style salmon and cod fishcakes with lime and ginger mayonnaise. The separate à la carte menu includes fish soup, spiced monkfish with tomato and lemon sauce, warm almond and pear tart with clotted cream.

Family facilities

Although there are few special facilities for children they are welcome indoors and the patio garden is a safe and pleasant spot for families to retreat to on fine days.

Alternative refreshment stops

The Old Passage Inn (which specialises in fresh fish) is on the riverbank to the west of Arlingham and passed on the walk. It has a riverside terrace but is more restaurant than pub.

☞ Where to go from here

The Wildfowl and Wetland Centre at Slimbridge (www.wwt.org.uk) is home to the world's largest collection of exotic wildfowl and up to 8,000 wild birds winter on the 200 acre (81ha) reserve of fields, marsh and mudflats on the River Severn. Berkeley Castle (www.berkeley-castle.com) is a rambling and romantic medieval fortress with terraced gardens and a beautiful butterfly house.

Bristol and Bath railway path

4

CYCLE

Bristol and Bath   BATH & N E SOMERSET

Park and ride with a difference, an easy ride to explore Bath's fine 18th-century architecture

Avon Valley Railway

The first section of the Avon Valley Railway opened in 1835, between Mangotsfield, just north of Warmley and Bristol. Originally a horse-drawn tramway, it transported local coal to Bristol. With growing industrialisation, the track was upgraded for steam and by 1869 had been extended all the way to Bath, following the course of the River Avon as it neared the city. After publication of the Beeching Report, passenger trains were withdrawn in March 1966, although goods traffic continued for a further five years, supplying coal to the gasworks in Bath. In 1972 the track was finally dismantled, but even as British Rail was removing the rails, the Bristol Suburban Railway Society was planning to reopen the line. A 2.5 mile (4km) section is now operational with extensions planned.

Known the world over for its Roman baths and elegant Cotswold-stone Georgian architecture, Bath simply demands exploration. Dedicated to the goddess Sulis, the baths were begun in the 1st century, the focus of a sophisticated city that thrived for nearly 400 years. After the Romans left, the baths were gradually forgotten and when Nash created his fashionable spa town, nobody even dreamed of their existence. The former complex was only rediscovered in 1880 when sewer works broke into the subterranean ruin, and subsequent excavation revealed the finest Roman remains in the country.

the ride

1 Leaving the car park adjacent to the former Warmley Station, go left to cross the main road at a traffic light controlled crossing and follow the path away beside the old signal box. Hidden behind the trees lining the path are small units, occupying the sites of the former industries that once supported the town. After passing beneath **St Ivel Way**, look for a sculpture that represents a Roman centurion quaffing wine from a flask: it recalls that a Roman road passed nearby. A little further along is a controlled crossing at **Victoria Road**.

2 Pedalling on brings you to **Oldland Common**, the northern terminus of the restored section of the Avon Valley Railway. The path continues beside the track, passing beneath North Street to enter a shallow cutting. The stone here, known as Pennant sandstone, is particularly hard and proved an excellent construction material. The excavated stone was used for several buildings in the vicinity. There are also coal deposits in the area, laid down during the same carboniferous period and these

Left: The former Warmley Station

Pulteney Bridge over the River Avon in Bath

fuelled local brass foundries and other industries. Later on, at **Cherry Gardens**, the way enters a second cutting, exposing much younger rocks containing fossils of graptolites, belemnites and ammonites, creatures that lived in the Jurassic seas covering the region 200 million years ago. Before long, the **railway yard** at Bitton appears ahead, the cycle track swinging across the line through a gate (look out for passing trains) to reach the station.

3 Even if the trains are not running, there is always something of interest to see in the goods yard, with an assortment of engines and rolling stock either awaiting refurbishment or dismantling for spares. The buffet is generally open and for a small donation you are welcome to wander onto the platform. Go through the car park, over a small level crossing and continue beside the railway. Carry on along an embankment overlooking the Avon's flood meadows, crossing the river to reach **Avon Riverside Station**, where a path on the right drops to a picnic area by the water's edge.

4 At **Saltford,** the Bird in Hand below the embankment invites a break for refreshment. You can also wander into the village and have a look at the restored **Saltford Brass Mill**, which is open on some Saturdays during the summer months. Re-crossing the river the way continues towards Bath, the Avon winding below you twice more before you reach the outskirts of the city.

5 Eventually you emerge on **Brassmill Lane**. Follow the road to the right, keeping ahead on a short cycle lane further

3h30 **18.25 MILES** **29.4 KM** **LEVEL 1**23

MAP: OS Explorer 155 Bristol & Bath
START/FINISH: car park beside the A420 at Warmley, Kingswood; grid ref: ST 670735
TRAILS/TRACKS: former railway line
LANDSCAPE: wooded cuttings and embankments with occasional views across riverside path into Bath
PUBLIC TOILETS: at car park at start
TOURIST INFORMATION: Bath, tel 01225 477101
CYCLE HIRE: Webbs of Warmley, High Street, Warmley, Bristol, tel 01179 673676
THE PUB: Bird in Hand, Saltford
🚦 Traffic lights control major road crossings; dismount when crossing the restored railway line; care when riding alongside the River Avon; route shared with pedestrians.

Getting to the start

Warmley is on the A420 to the east of Bristol. The car park lies 0.25 mile (400m) east of the roundabout junction with the A4174.

Why do this cycle ride

Bath is notorious for its traffic problems. For the cyclist, however, there is a splendid route along the track bed of the former Avon Valley Railway. It penetrates the heart of the city and has attractions of its own along the way: you can visit a brass mill, or ride along a section of the line, pulled by a vintage steam or diesel engine. The cycling is not strenuous, but for a shorter ride, turn around at Saltford.

Researched and written by: Dennis Kelsall

on past a 'no entry' sign for motorised traffic. Where the cycle lane ends, turn right (watch for oncoming traffic) to gain a riverside path behind a tool hire shop. Signed towards **Bath city centre**, keep going past the 19th-century industrial quarter of Bath, where more brass and other mills took advantage of the water for both power and transport. The factories have now gone, replaced by modern light industry, but some of the old riverside

warehouses remain. The path finally ends near **Churchill Bridge** in the centre of Bath.

6 Although cyclists are common on Bath's streets, the traffic is busy and it is perhaps a good idea to find a convenient spot to secure your bikes whilst you explore on foot. When you are ready to head back, retrace your outward route to **Warmley** along the riverside path and cycleway.

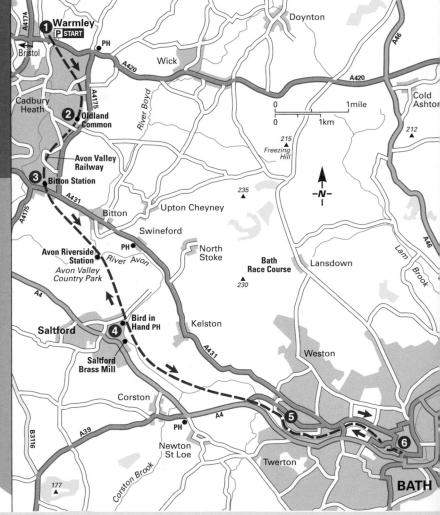

Bird in Hand

Converted in 1869 from two cottages in the original village close to the River Avon, the Bird in Hand first served the workers building the railway through the valley between Bath and Bristol. Now that the railway has gone, this homely village local, which is smack beside the old route, is a favoured resting and refuelling stop for cyclists pedalling the peaceful cycle path between the two cities. There's a comfortable bar area adorned with old pictures of the pub and village, a light and airy conservatory and plenty of outdoor seating for fine-weather eating and drinking.

Food

Lunchtime food ranges from Stilton ploughman's and salad platters to steak and ale pies, omelettes and ham, egg and chips. Evening additions include a mixed grill and daily specials such as salmon fishcakes, sea bass with prawn and lemon butter sauce, dressed crab and rack of lamb with redcurrant and port sauce.

Family facilities

Children are very welcome inside. There's a family area with a box of toys to keep youngsters amused, and a basic children's menu.

Alternative refreshment stops

Range of pubs and cafés in Bath; café at Bitton Station.

☛ Where to go from here

Spend time in Bath visiting the Abbey, the Roman Baths and Pump Rooms (www.romanbaths.co.uk) or the excellent museums (www.bath-preservation-trust.org.uk). In Bristol head for the superb Zoo Gardens (www.bristolzoo.org.uk) or savour the unique sights, sounds and smells of steam trains along the Avon Valley Railway at Bitton (www.avonvalleyrailway.co.uk).

about the pub

Bird in Hand
58 High Street
Saltford, Bristol
BS31 3EN
Tel: 01225 873335

DIRECTIONS: 3 miles (4.8km) along the cycle track from Bitton railway station
PARKING: 36
OPEN: daily
FOOD: daily
BREWERY/COMPANY: free house
REAL ALE: Abbey Bellringer, Butcombe, Courage Best, guest beers

Severnside at Ashleworth and Hasfield

A fine walk along the banks of the River Severn, visiting a huge and beautifully preserved tithe barn.

Medieval taxes and tithe barns

Medieval tithe barns, such as the impressive example at Ashleworth, still survive around the country in surprisingly large numbers. They date back to the period before the 16th century, when the great monasteries owned much of the land that was not held by the Crown. Around

Ashleworth the land belonged to Bristol Abbey. The local people who worked the land were tenants who, in return for working the land, were allowed access to common land and also to work some fields for themselves.

They were obliged to pay tithes, or taxes, to the abbey. This was most often in the form of produce, stored in the tithe barn, which usually stood close to the church and the abbot's residence. The presence of a huge tithe barn here, in what today is a comparatively remote village, has a geographical explanation. Ashleworth is

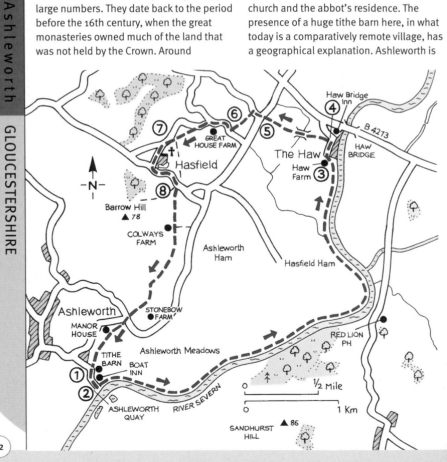

situated at an easily fordable part of the river – an important consideration before the era of easy transportation. There had been a church at Ashleworth since before the compilation of the Domesday Book. A manor house certainly existed during the Norman period, and no doubt before. The barn, and Ashleworth Court next to it, date from the late 15th century.

The limestone barn is 125ft (38m) long, consisting of ten bays – a huge building by any standards. Had you wandered through the barn 500 years ago you would have seen different types of grain, honey, dairy produce and, of course, Cotswold wool, all of which would have been subsequently shipped downriver. Ashleworth Court, next door, is a fine example of a medieval stone building, barely changed since the time of its construction.

the walk

1 From the **Tithe Barn**, walk along the lane towards the River Severn, passing The Boat Inn on your left-hand side.

2h45 — 6.5 MILES — 10.5 KM — LEVEL 1 2 3

MAP: OS Explorer 179 Gloucester, Cheltenham & Stroud
START/FINISH: Ashleworth Quay: Very limited parking on grass verges in the vicinity of the Tithe Barn; grid ref: SO 818251
PATHS: tracks, fields, lanes and riverbank, 21 stiles
LANDSCAPE: flat: river, meadows, woods, farms, villages and distant hills
PUBLIC TOILETS: none on route
TOURIST INFORMATION: Gloucester, tel 01452 396572
THE PUB: The Boat Inn, Ashleworth

Getting to the start

Ashleworth is 5 miles (8km) north of Gloucester close to the western bank of the River Severn. The village is signed from the A417 at Hartpury. There is parking for a small number of cars by the tithe barn (National Trust) on the lane leading to the Quay. Ensure you do not impede traffic or obstruct gateways.

Researched and written by:
Dennis Kelsall, Christopher Knowles

Above: The old Tithe Barn at Ashleworth
Previous page: Ashleworth Manor House

2 Turn left over a stile to walk along the riverbank. Follow it for a little over 3 miles (4.8km). In general the path is obvious, but where it sometimes appears to pass through gates that are locked, you should instead use a stile, usually found to the right. **Sandhurst Hill** will come and go across the river, followed by the Red Lion pub, sadly also out of reach.

3 Eventually you will pass a house, **Haw Farm**. Immediately after it follow a track that swings away from the river and then passes several half-timbered houses and cottages. It soon develops as a lane and **Haw Bridge** appears before you.

4 Approaching the pub, where the lane splits, leave over a stile on the left into a field. Walk straight on, but then as the field opens up, bear half left to a gate in the far corner. Through it, go forward a few paces, turn right to cross a bridge and then continue straight on across two more fields.

5 Emerging onto a junction of lanes, cross to walk down the one opposite, signed **Tirley Hill**. However, after 30yds (27m), turn over a plank bridge and stile concealed in the hedge on the left. Cross the field, aiming for a gateway about half-way along the right-hand hedge. Maintain the same line in the next field, exiting through a gateway onto a lane.

what to look for

The River Severn can flood quite badly and you will notice a number of damage limitation devices built in the vicinity of Ashleworth and elsewhere. In the past floods have reached as far as the church every two or three years. The worst flood, however, was in 1947. The level the water reached is recorded on the wall of the south aisle.

6 Walk right and pass **Great House Farm**, staying with the lane as it later winds left up the hill. After passing two houses, cross left into a field. Head downhill to the far-right corner and rejoin the lane.

7 Turn left and continue into **Hasfield**, keeping left for Ashleworth. **Hasfield Church** is then signed off left opposite a telephone box, and if you go to have a look, return to the main lane. Carry on through the village, keeping left again at the next junction, still heading towards Ashleworth.

8 After 0.25 mile (400m), look for a waymarked track into a field on the right beside a small post box and **flood depth marker**. Follow the perimeter track, but leave it over a stile on the left, just after entering the second field. Continue parallel with the track in the adjacent enclosure. Keep forward past **Colways Farm** to a kissing gate on the right just beyond the buildings. Pass through and go left beside the hedge. In the next field, strike a diagonal to the far corner and, over a bridge there, bear half left across. Over more stiles, cross an overgrown track and head towards the base of a pylon, passing **Stonebow Farm**, lying over to the left. Carry on to a last stile and escape onto a lane. In the corner of the junction, diagonally left, return to the fields over yet another stile. Make for a gap in the far corner and keep ahead at the field-edge, finally returning to the **tithe barn**.

The Boat Inn

With historic connections to King Charles who granted ferry rights to the pub, The Boat stands beside Ashleworth Quay and close by the medieval Tithe Barn and former Court House. In the same family since the pub was licensed by royal charter in the 17th century, it's a gem of a pub with its tiny front parlour, flagstone floors, old scrubbed tables, fireside chairs, ancient kitchen range and time-honoured pub games; a magnet to the many walkers exploring the nearby Severn or the village itself (leaflets available from the bar). Interesting real ales from local micro-breweries are dispensed direct from the cask and change daily. They are ideal to accompany perhaps a generously filled roll or ploughman's lunch with pickle. There is plenty of seating outside to enjoy the location. Come for the annual beer festival in late summer.

about the pub

The Boat Inn

The Quay, Ashleworth
Gloucester, Gloucestershire GL19 4HZ
Tel: 01452 700272

DIRECTIONS: beside the quay just south of the tithe barn

PARKING: 10

OPEN: closed Monday & Wednesday lunchtime in summer; all day Monday, and Wednesday & Thursday lunchtime in winter

FOOD: lunchtimes only

BREWERY/COMPANY: free house

REAL ALE: 4 changing micro-brewery beers

DOGS: allowed in garden only

Family facilities

Children are welcome until 8pm. Lovely courtyard garden for summer drinking.

Alternative refreshment stops

There is also a pub just off the route on the other side of the B4213 at Haw Bridge (unsurprisingly the Haw Bridge Inn), or you could try the Queen's Arms in Ashleworth village.

☞ Where to go from here

The Shambles Victorian Village in Newent has cobbled streets, alleyways and cottages set in over an acre (0.4ha) with display shops and trades. At the National Birds of Prey Centre near Newent, there are over 110 aviaries on view with 85 species, and birds are flown daily.

Food

Bar food is limited to excellent lunchtime ploughman's or rolls filled with home-cooked ham and mustard, cheese and pickle, salmon and cucumber, or egg and cress.

Stroud Valley cycle trail

Stroud Valley

GLOUCESTERSHIRE

Explore Cotswold's industrial heritage along a disused railway track.

Nailsworth valley

Throughout the medieval period, wool was an important product of the Cotswolds, much of it traded abroad as fleeces. However, it was only during the 17th century that workers around Stroud began to exploit the fast-flowing streams to power washing, dyeing and fulling mills. The valleys prospered as new inventions mechanised the spinning and weaving processes during the 18th century, and the canals, followed by the railways, provided

a ready means of exporting the finished goods via the seaport of Bristol. At one time there were 15 mills spaced along the valley between Stonehouse and Nailsworth, but the age of steam, which initially contributed to their success, also heralded their gradual decline. The mills struggled to compete with the massive steam-driven factories on the coal fields of Lancashire and Yorkshire, and although some were modernised, the long-term cost of bringing in fuel proved uneconomic.

While operated as part of the Midland network, the Nailsworth Railway was completed in 1867 after 3 years' construction. It encouraged diversification of the mills into other products such as pin

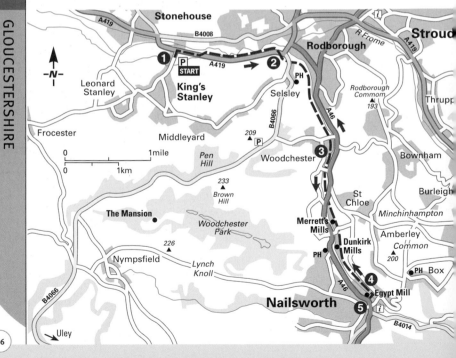

making, carpet manufacture, dye making and, of course, grain milling. One of the valley's more unusual products, walking sticks, are made from chestnut saplings, and the trade continues today, with Nailsworth claiming to be the largest producer in the world.

the ride

1 Leaving the car park, cross the King's Stanley road and then the A419 at the traffic lights. The **cycle way** runs briefly along the pavement in the direction of Dudbridge and Stroud, crossing another traffic light controlled junction at the entrance to a **small trading estate** – look both ways as you cross. Not far beyond, the track and road separate, the way continuing in pleasant seclusion between broad hedges. Breaks on the left allow occasional glimpses across the Frome valley, where meadows lie between the twisting river and the disused Stroudwater Canal. The route here is also a **miniature arboretum**, planted with intriguingly named varieties of apple and pear trees such as The Gillyflower of Gloucester, Chaxhill Red, Elison's Orange and Blakeney Red, developed during the 19th century for cider and perry manufacture as well as just for eating.

2 After a mile (1.6km), the track swings to cross the A419 next to the **Dudbridge roundabout** at pedestrian-controlled traffic lights. Go left on the far side, now following signs for Nailsworth, skirting the roundabout and entering a tunnel below the B4066. Keep ahead as you come out on the other side, the tree-lined track winding into the **Nailsworth Valley**. The stream that

2h00 **9.5 MILES** **15.3 KM** **LEVEL 123**

MAP: OS Explorer 168 Stroud, Tetbury & Malmesbury

START/FINISH: car park beside A419 at King's Stanley; grid ref: SO 814044

TRAILS/TRACKS: firm track

LANDSCAPE: disused railway track following the course of the River Frome and the Nailsworth Valley

PUBLIC TOILETS: none on route

TOURIST INFORMATION: Nailsworth, tel 01453 839222

CYCLE HIRE: None locally

THE PUB: Egypt Mill, Nailsworth

🛑 Major road crossings controlled by traffic lights, shared with pedestrians

Getting to the start

Stroud is 8 miles (12.9km) south of Gloucester. The ride begins from a car park at the edge of Stonehouse beside a junction on the A419, where an unclassified road leaves south to King's Stanley.

Why do this cycle ride?

The deep, steep-sided valleys converging on Stroud have a very different character to the rolling wolds further north. Canals and railways guaranteed prosperity into the 19th century, providing ready access to formerly remote areas. This easy ride follows the course of the former Nailsworth Railway from Stonehouse, at one time lined with a succession of busy mills.

Researched and written by:
Dennis Kelsall, Christopher Knowles

Stroud Valley

GLOUCESTERSHIRE

powered the many mills along its course runs beside you, seemingly altogether too insignificant for the work demanded from it. Its force was concentrated by damming small ponds or lodges at intervals. Look out for a sudden dip where a bridge over a crossing track has been removed, then after passing beneath a bridge, go over a residential street.

3 The track shortly crosses **Nailsworth Stream**, then briefly runs beside the main road before reaching Station Road. There is little to mark the former station as the trail continues, in a little distance passing beneath the main road and then beside **Merrett's Mills**, now occupied by industrial units. As the railings finish beyond it, keep an eye open for a small

bridge taking the track over a narrow path. The path, reached on the left just after crossing, provides pedestrian access to **Dunkirk Mills**. Although now largely converted to residential accommodation, it houses a small museum, which is occasionally open in summer and contains working machinery from the former textile mill. The track continues through trees along the valley, past the lodges that created a head of water for driving the mill wheels, and eventually reaches a residential development and car park at **Goldwater Springs**.

4 Follow the access drive out to the left, swinging right to follow a lane past a fire station. Just before crossing a bridge to meet the main road into Nailsworth, go right again into **Egypt Mill**. Another of the valley's former industrial mills, it is enjoying a new career as a hotel. Inside, it retains two original mill wheels and their gearing in working order, and they can be seen from the basement bars, turning in the flow.

5 In the past, the abrupt sides of the valley kept Nailsworth relatively isolated from the outside world. This means that, without tackling the steep hills onto Minchinhampton Common, the only return is back the way you came.

The river near Egypt Mill prettily surrounded by bushes, plants and trees

Egypt Mill

about the pub

Egypt Mill
Nailsworth, Stroud
Gloucestershire GL6 0AE
Tel: 01453 833449

DIRECTIONS: first right at roundabout, then left on leaving the A46 heading north out of Nailsworth towards Stroud

PARKING: 60

OPEN: daily; all day

FOOD: daily

BREWERY/COMPANY: free house

REAL ALE: Archer's Best; guest beer in summer

ROOMS: 17 en suite

Situated in the charming Cotswold town of Nailsworth, this smartly converted 16th-century corn mill contains many features of great character, including two working water wheels, the original millstones and lifting equipment. The refurbished, split-level ground floor bar and bistro are informal, offering a relaxing atmosphere and super views of the water wheels and over the pretty millstream to the peaceful water gardens. The large and very comfortable Egypt Mill Lounge sports stripped beams and old mill machinery ironwork.
There's a choice of eating in the bistro or restaurant, and in both there is a good selection of wines by the glass. Bedrooms are well equipped and tastefully furnished.

Food
Light lunches range from sandwiches and ciabatta rolls (bacon and Brie) served with salad and crisps, risottos and salads, cheeses and cold meats, pasta dishes and local sausages and mash. The main menu may take in starters such as deep-fried spicy crab cakes, smoked salmon, or portobello mushrooms, followed by confit of duck leg, deep-fried haddock or steak and kidney suet pudding. Round off with butterscotch tart or dark chocolate and marshmallow cheesecake.

Family facilities
Children are very welcome in the bars and overnight (family room with cots). There's a children's menu and plenty of summer seating in the riverside gardens, where young children must be supervised.

Alternative refreshment stops
Choice of pubs in Nailsworth.

☛ Where to go from here
See working machinery and historical displays at the Dunkirk Mill Centre, a fulling mill demonstrating the finishing of fine woollen cloth (www.stroud-textile.org.uk). View dinosaur remains and a Roman temple at the Museum in the Park in Stroud (www.stroud.gov.uk). Explore Owlpen Manor, a romantic Tudor manor with formal yew gardens (www.owlpen.com) or the unfinished Woodchester Mansion (www.woodchestermansion.org.uk).

A walk around Box Hill

A hilly walk around Box Hill, famous for its stone and Brunel's greatest engineering achievement.

Brunel's famous tunnel

Box is a large straggling village that sits astride the busy A4 half-way between Bath and Chippenham. Stone has been quarried here since the 9th century, but Box found fame during the 18th century when the local stone was used for Bath's magnificent buildings. Construction of Box Tunnel uncovered immense deposits of stone and by 1900 Box stone quarries were among the world's most productive. Little trace remains above ground, except for some fine stone-built houses in the village and a few reminders of the industry on Box Hill.

In 1833, the newly created Great Western Railway appointed Isambard Kingdom Brunel (1806–59) as engineer. His task was to build a railway covering the 118 miles (190km) from London to Bristol. The problems and projects he encountered on the way would help to make him the most famous engineer of the Victorian age. After a relatively straightforward and level start through the Home Counties, which earned the nickname 'Brunel's Billiard Table', he came to the hilly Cotswolds.

The solution at Box would be a tunnel, and at nearly 2 miles (3.2km) long and with a gradient of 1:100 it would be the longest and steepest in the world at the time. It would also be very wide. Already controversial, Brunel ignored the gauge of other companies, preferring the 7ft (2.1m) used by tramways and roads. He also made the tunnel dead straight.

All was on a grand scale: a ton of gunpowder and candles was used every week, 3 million bricks were fired to line the soft Cotswold limestone and 100 workers lost their lives. Although Brunel would ultimately lose the battle of the gauges, his magnificent line meant that Bristol was then a mere two hours from the capital.

the walk

1 Facing the recreation ground, walk to the far left-hand corner of the playing field, leaving by a track close to the railway line. When you reach the lane, turn left, pass beneath the railway, cross a bridge and take the arrowed **footpath**, to the right, before the second bridge.

A shaded walk near Box Hill

A cricket match on Box Common – a typical village scene

2 Walk beside the river, cross a footbridge and turn right. Cross a further footbridge and continue to a stile. Walk through **water meadows** close to the river, go through a squeeze stile and maintain direction. Towards the far end, bear left to a squeeze stile in the field corner. Follow the right-hand field-edge to a stile and lane.

3 Turn right, then right again at the junction. Cross the river, pass **Drewett's Mill** and steeply ascend the lane. At a bend, just past **Mills Platt Farm**, take the left-most of the two arrowed footpaths ahead across a stile. Continue steeply uphill to a stile and, with care, cross the A4. Ascend steps to a lane and proceed straight on up **Barnetts Hill**. Keep right at the fork, then right again and pass the Quarryman's Arms.

4 Keep left at the fork and continue beside **Box Hill Common** to a triangle junction. Bear right and cross to take the path straight ahead into woodland. Almost immediately, fork left and follow the path close to the woodland edge. Later, as it curves right into the beech wood, keep ahead and then bear left, leaving the trees through a gap in the wall. Immediately go right at the junction of paths.

5 Follow the bridle path, eventually reaching a fork. Keep ahead, then after a few paces turn right at a T-junction. At once, take a path left to a stile. Cross a further stile and descend into **Thorn Wood**, following the stepped path to a stile at the bottom.

1h15 — **3.25 MILES** — **5.3 KM** — **LEVEL 1 2 3**

MAP: OS Explorer 156 Chippenham & Bradford-on-Avon

START/FINISH: Box: village car park near Selwyn Hall; grid ref: ST 823686

PATHS: field and woodland paths, bridleways, lanes, 18 stiles

LANDSCAPE: river valley and wooded hillsides

PUBLIC TOILETS: opposite Queens Head in Box

TOURIST INFORMATION: Bath, tel 01225 477101

THE PUB: The Quarryman's Arms, Box Hill

Getting to the start

Box is 5.5 miles (8.9km) east of Bath where the A361 meets the A4. However, if approaching from the south along the A361, note there is no right turn onto the A4; you must go right at an earlier sign to Chippenham (A4) and then left along the A4. Parking is beside Selwyn Hall playing fields, signed off the main road.

Researched and written by:
David Hancock, Dennis Kelsall

what to look for

Explore Box and locate the Blind House on the main street, one of a dozen in Wiltshire for disturbers of the peace. Look for Coleridge House, named after the poet who often broke his journey here on his way to Nether Stowey. Also look for the former candle factory on the Rudloe road, which once produced the candles used during the building of Box Tunnel, and head east along the A4 for the best view of the tunnel's entrance.

6 Continue through scrub to a stile and turn right beside the fence to a wall stile. Bear right to a further stile, then bear left uphill to a stile and the A361. Cross over and follow the drive ahead. Where it curves left by stables, keep ahead along the

arrowed path to a house. Ignore the stepped garden path and go to the rear corner of the house, there swinging right up a contained path that leads to a lane at the top.

7 Turn left, then just before the houses of **Henley**, take a path right, across a stile. Follow the field-edge to a stile and descend to an allotment and stile. Continue to a stile and gate.

8 Walk on towards the buildings in front, looking for a contained path dropping between them, a little to the left. Cross the A361 to another alley opposite, taking care at the bottom as you emerge directly onto the busy A4. Turn right, then left down the access road back to **Selwyn Hall**.

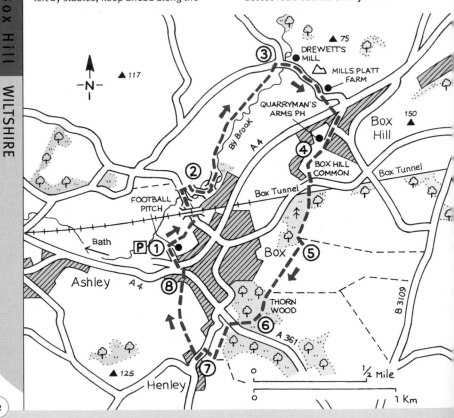

The Quarryman's Arms

Time your walk according to opening time at The Quarryman's Arms, a 300-year-old pub tucked away up a narrow hillside lane with quite splendid views over the Colerne Valley. This rustic rural local is also on the Macmillan Way long-distance footpath, providing accommodation and luggage transfer, and has long been a favoured watering-hole with walkers, cavers, potholers and local cyclists. The pleasantly modernised bar is packed with mining-related memorabilia and photographs as it was the local ale house of the Bath stone miners, and you can hear and feel the trains taking trips down the old stone mines. So why not enjoy the views across Box from the dining room with a hearty lunch and a pint of locally brewed ale, just like the stone miners once did.

Food

From the extensive snack menu tuck into ham, egg and chips, thick-cut sandwiches, fish and chips or a Quarryman's platter (ham, cheddar, Stilton with home-made pickle, salad and farmhouse bread). From the main menu try the Stilton and asparagus pancake, the ever-popular steak and ale pie, poached salmon, or lamb shank with mint and rosemary sauce.

Family facilities

Children are very welcome inside the pub. There's a family room, a children's menu, small portions of adult dishes, high chairs and baby-changing facilities. Supervision is required in the small garden.

Alternative refreshment stops

In Box, you will find both the Queen's Head and The Bear offer good food and ale in convivial surroundings.

☛ Where to go from here

Visit Haselbury Manor at Wadswick for its restored landscaped gardens. Learn more about the Bath stone quarrying industry through a visit to the heritage centre in nearby Corsham. In the centre of town is Corsham Court, an Elizabethan manor that was home to the Methuen family, which contains fine furniture and paintings.

about the pub

The Quarryman's Arms

Box Hill, Box, Corsham
Wiltshire SN13 8HN
Tel: 01225 743569
www.quarrymans-arms.co.uk

DIRECTIONS: A4 east of Box, turn right into Bargates before railway bridge, then at T-junction turn left up Quarry Hill. Left again at junction by grassy area, left after hotel into Beech Road, then third left into Barnetts Hill. At top of hill turn right to reach the pub

PARKING: 25

OPEN: daily; all day Friday, Saturday & Sunday

FOOD: daily

BREWERY/COMPANY: free house

REAL ALE: Butcombe Bitter, Wadworth 6X, Moles Bitter

DOGS: welcome in the pub

ROOMS: 3 bedrooms (2 en suite)

From Bradford-on-Avon along the Kennet & Avon Canal

Discover one of Brindley's great canal masterpieces.

Kennet & Avon Canal

John Rennie began the construction of the Kennet and Avon Canal in 1794 to link the Avon and Kennet Navigations between Bath and Bristol and thus create a continuous waterway between Bristol and London. The 57 mile (92km) canal took 16 years to complete and was quite an achievement, requiring two great aqueducts and a spectacular flight of 29 locks at Caen Hill outside Devizes to lift the waterway over 240ft (73m) onto the summit level. It proved a highly profitable venture and was soon carrying over 350,000 tons a year between the two great cities. By the middle of the 19th century, competition from railways foreshadowed its decline, and in 1846 was taken over by the Great Western Railway Company. GWR signs remain on some of its bridges, ominously mounted on the instrument of its ruin, an upended length of railway track. Re-opened in 1990, many of the canal's original features still excite the imagination, none more so than the two splendid stone aqueducts carrying the canal across the Avon Valley, one of them named after the canal company's founding chairman, Charles Dundas. They presented major technical difficulties for Rennie as they had not only to carry a great weight but remain watertight, yet his

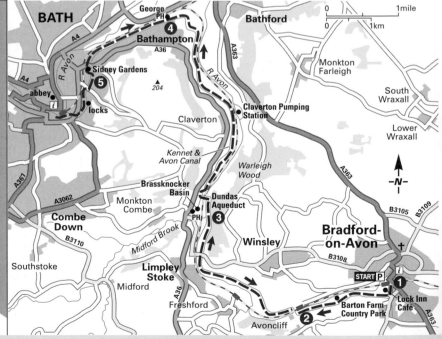

Dundas Aqueduct where the Kennet and Avon Canal turns sharply

4h00 — **20 MILES** — **32.2 KM** — **LEVEL 1**23

SHORTER ALTERNATIVE ROUTE

3h00 — **15 MILES** — **24.1 KM** — **LEVEL 1**23

MAP: OS Explorer 155 Bristol & Bath & 156 Chippenham & Bradford-on-Avon

START/FINISH: Bradford-on-Avon railway station (pay car park); grid ref: ST 825606

TRAILS/TRACKS: gravel tow path, short section on road

LANDSCAPE: canal tow path through the wooded and pastoral Avon Valley

PUBLIC TOILETS: at start

TOURIST INFORMATION: Bradford-on-Avon, tel 01225 865797

CYCLE HIRE: The Lock Inn Café, 48 Frome Road, Bradford-on-Avon tel: 01225 868068

THE PUB: The George, Bathampton

🛈 Care through town; unguarded canal tow paths shared with pedestrians; blind approaches to bridges; dismount in tunnels; flight of steps on approaching Bath

Getting to the start
Bradford-on-Avon is only 5 miles (8km) south east of Bath and lies on the A363 to Trowbridge. Park at the railway station, from where the ride begins.

Why do this cycle ride?
The Kennet and Avon Canal passes through picturesque countryside. An attractive riverside pub at Bathampton offers a turning point although the locks passed into Bath on the longer ride are worth seeing.

Researched and written by: Dennis Kelsall

creations combined both aesthetic quality and practicality in the best tradition of the great architects.

the ride

1 Leaving the station car park, turn right along the main road in the direction of Frome. Continue past a mini-roundabout to the Canal Tavern and Lock Inn Café. Go between them to join the towpath and follow it past **Grange Farm** with its massive 600-year-old tithe barn. The River Avon runs below to the right, containing Barton Farm Country Park's picnic and wildlife areas within the intervening spit of land. Beyond a gate, continue beside the canal to **Avoncliff**.

2 The canal now makes an abrupt turn across the Avon Valley, carried above both the river and railway on an imposing aqueduct. Do not cross, but at a sign to Dundas just before, drop steeply right towards the **Cross Guns** pub, then double back left underneath the bridge, climbing left to gain the opposite towpath. Tacked along the wooded valley, the waterway runs pleasantly on, harbouring an assortment of ducks, coots and moorhens. Turning a corner opposite **Limpley Stoke**, pass beneath a road bridge, then look out on the left for a glimpse of a viaduct taking the A36 across the Midford Brook valley.

Taking life at a leisurely pace along the canal

3 Another sharp turn heralds the **Dundas Aqueduct**, immediately beyond which is the last remnant of the Somerset Coal Canal, completed in 1805 to transport coal from Radstock and Paulton to Bristol. The track just before it leads to **Brassknocker Basin**, where a small exhibition (open daily in summer) describes its history. The route, however, continues ahead, signed 'Bath and Claverton', winding behind a **derrick** and maintenance building and onto the opposite bank. A mile (1.2km) further on, immediately beyond a bridge, a track drops across the railway to the river where there is a restored pump house (**Claverton Pumping Station**), built in 1813 to replenish the water drained by the locks descending to Bath. There are views to Bathford and Batheaston as you pedal the last 1.75 miles (2.8km) to **Bathampton** and The George.

4 To extend the ride, continue beside the canal, the eastern suburbs of Bath rising on the opposite side of the valley. Eventually the city itself comes into view with a glimpse of the abbey at its heart. There are a couple of short tunnels to pass through at **Sidney Gardens**, where you

should dismount. Between them, two **ornate cast-iron bridges** span the canal, which, together with the elaborate façade of the second tunnel beneath Cleveland House, were added to placate the owners of Sidney Park, who rather disapproved of common cargo barges passing through their land.

5 Emerging below **Cleveland House**, the towpath doubles back onto the opposite bank, passes former warehouses, now a **marina**, and rises to a road. Taking care, diagonally cross and drop back to the tow path, here having to negotiate a flight of steps. Beyond, the canal falls impressively through a succession of locks, the path periodically rising to cross a couple of roads and a track before meeting the River Avon. To explore Bath, carry on a little further by the river to emerge on the road beside **Churchill Bridge** in the city centre. As the city is busy, it is perhaps preferable to secure your bikes whilst you wander around. The return is back the way you came, but remember you have to climb steps to the road at Bathwick Hill and dismount through the tunnels at Sidney Gardens, or you could return by train.

The George

The pub's enviable position by the parish church and a bridge over the Kennet and Avon Canal is one of its attractions. The creeper-clad building is so close to the water that the entrance to the upper dining room is from the tow path. When the weather is fine, the tables on the canalside terrace fill quickly with walkers, cyclists and barge visitors, and you can watch the many activities on the canal. Inside, there's a warren of wood-beamed rooms radiating out from the flagstoned central bar, with plenty of space away from the bar for families. The George oozes history, dating back to the 13th century when it was originally a monastery. The last official duel in England was fought on nearby Claverton Down in 1778 following a quarrel over a game of cards at The George. The fatally wounded Viscount du Barré was buried in the churchyard opposite.

Food

Expect traditional pub food – sandwiches and filled rolls (roast beef and horseradish), salads, ploughman's lunches, and changing blackboard specials, perhaps roast monkfish, steak and kidney pudding or Tuscan-style swordfish.

Family facilities

Children are welcome away from the bar and a children's menu is available. Keep an eye on children on the canalside terrace.

Alternative refreshment stops

Plenty of eating places in Bradford-on-Avon and Bath. The Lock Inn Café near the start, the Cross Guns at Avoncliff, the Hop Pole and a canalside tea room at Limpley Stoke.

☛ Where to go from here

Take a closer look at the tithe barn and seek out the unspoiled Saxon church in Bradford-on-Avon. Visit the Claverton Pumping Station (www.claverton.org) or explore Bath's famous buildings and museums (www.bath-preservation-trust.org.uk). Peto Gardens at Iford Manor (www.ifordarts.co.uk) are worth seeing.

about the pub

The George
Mill Lane
Bathampton, Bath
Bath & NE Somerset BA2 6TR
Tel: 01225 425079

DIRECTIONS: at Bathampton on the A36 east of Bath, take minor road left downhill to village centre, crossing the canal to the church. The George is beside the canal near the church

PARKING: 50

OPEN: daily; all day

FOOD: daily; all day

BREWERY/COMPANY: Chef & Brewer

REAL ALE: Wadworth 6X, Courage Best & Directors, Greene King Old Speckled Hen

Painswick and Washpool Valley

From the Queen of the Cotswolds through the Washpool Valley.

Time-honoured traditions

Local traditions continue to thrive in Painswick, the 'Queen of the Cotswolds'. These are centred around its well-known churchyard which is famously filled, not only with the 'table' tombs of 18th-century clothiers, but also with 99 beautifully manicured yew trees, planted in 1792. The legend is that only 99 ever grow, as Old Nick will kill off the hundredth.

This tale has become confused with an ancient 'clipping' ceremony that still takes place here in mid-September. This derives from the Saxon word 'clyping', meaning 'embrace', and is used in conjunction with the church. Children join hands to form a circle around the church or churchyard, and advance and retreat to and from the church, singing the *Clipping Hymn*. The children wear flowers in their hair and are rewarded with a coin and a bun for their efforts.

Cooper's Hill is the scene of cheese-rolling on Spring Bank Holidays when some folk slither precariously down the steep hill in pursuit of a 'cheese'. The winner receives a real cheese.

the walk

1 Leaving Painswick car park climb right along the main street, passing The Falcon Inn opposite the church. Turn left into **Gloucester Street**, the B4073, keeping ahead as it later joins another road. After 0.25 mile (400m), and just before a speed derestriction sign, go right onto **Golf Course**

Road. Shortly bear left through a small car park, but instead of rejoining the lane beyond, swing left on a track, signed 'Cotswold Way and Painswick Beacon'. Almost immediately fork right on a path at the edge of trees, continuing ahead across the **golf course** (look out for flying golf balls) and a narrow lane.

2 Pass left of a cemetery, concealed behind a low wall and trees, then cross another fairway to a wood. Carry on, later joining a quarry track to a lane. Go left and then almost immediately right, climbing at the left edge of more golf course to pass a trig point on **Painswick Hill**. Descending beyond, pick up a path and then a track that falls left to regain the B4073.

3 Turn right, but after 100yds (91m), opposite a bus stop, bear off left along a path through the trees. Emerging onto the bend of a lane, go sharp left on a descending waymarked track. Keep ahead to **Spoonbed Farm**, passing the farmhouse to a gate and carry on at the edge of trees to a field track. Part-way along the second field, before a large ash, slip across the boundary to continue in the adjacent field. Over a stile in the corner, drop through a young plantation and walk past a power-cable post in the middle of the next field. Leave at the corner by **Upper Holcombe Farm** to a lane.

4 Turn left, shortly passing Holcombe House and then rising to a sharp bend at **Holcombe Farm**. Leave on a track ahead, but just after it swings right, mount a stile beside a gate on the left and follow the left boundary away. In the next field bear

Left: The Cotswold Way, Painswick Beacon
Below: Golf course on the Cotswold Way

3h45 — 7.25 MILES — 0.00 KM — LEVEL 123

right to a stile in the middle of the end hedge, then follow a hedged path downhill. Over a bridge spanning a stream, take the rightmost of two paths, climbing into a field to continue up its left edge.

5 Emerging at the top corner, walk out to a track, and follow it left down to **Edge Farm**. Approaching the yard gate, bear right beside the farmhouse to a gate. Cross an unkempt meadow to another gate, continuing at the edge of the next field to **Parkhurst Farm**. Keep ahead past cottages, joining a track out to a lane. Turn up the hill, leaving after 250yds (229m) opposite a house over a stile on the left. Bear half right across to another stile, where a path leads behind gardens into **Edge**.

6 Turn left, then sharp right, dropping past the village hall to **Edge Hill Farm**. Just before the farmhouse, leave over a stile on the left. Go left to a second stile, negotiate a muddy stream and follow the left hedge downfield. Across a bridge, climb ahead and, over successive stiles, maintain your course to a gate. Cross a track to a second gate and swing left, leaving the field corner onto Jenkin's Lane. A few paces left, bear off right on a track into a field. Keep ahead from field to field, a track finally leading you past houses to a lane by **Wragg Castle Farm**.

7 Walk down to the busy main road, crossing with care to **Pincot Lane** opposite. Follow it for 0.25 mile (400m) down to **Painswick Stream** and up the hill to a group of cottages. Over a stile on the left, strike out across a field, dipping across a small, wooded valley to continue to

MAP: OS Explorer 179 Gloucester, Cheltenham & Stroud

START/FINISH: Painswick: car park (pay and display) near library, just off main road; grid ref: SO 865095

PATHS: fields, tracks, golf course and a green lane, 29 stiles

LANDSCAPE: hills, valleys, villages, isolated farmhouses, extensive views

PUBLIC TOILETS: at car park

TOURIST INFORMATION: Stroud, tel 01453 760960

THE PUB: The Falcon Inn, Painswick

Getting to the start

Some 3 miles (4.8km) north of Stroud, Painswick is on the A46 at its junction with the B4073 from Gloucester. The car park is beside the main road towards the southern end of the village by the library.

Researched and written by:
Dennis Kelsall, Christopher Knowles

WALK

Painswick

GLOUCESTERSHIRE

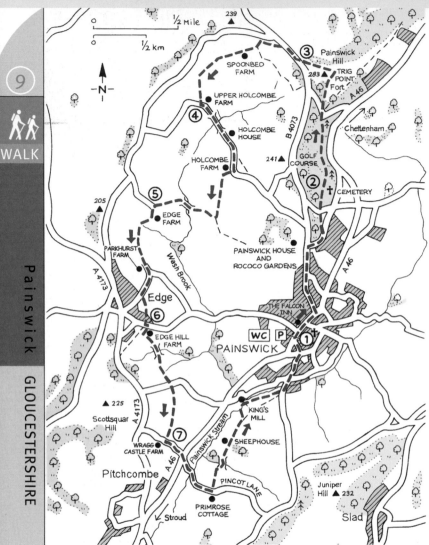

Sheephouse. Leave along the main drive, then bear left where it forks down to **King's Mill**. Through a gate on the right, cross the mill-pond dam and follow the stream at the field edge then along a contained path to emerge onto a lane. Go left and keep ahead as it climbs steeply for 0.33 mile (500m) back into **Painswick**.

what to look for

Just before you leave the golf course, at the highest point of the walk, you should be able to identify the ramparts and ditches of a hill fort beneath your feet. Like many such features on the Cotswold escarpment, this one is believed to date back to the Iron Age.

The Falcon Inn

Boasting the world's oldest-known bowling green in its grounds, The Falcon dates from 1554 and stands at the heart of a conservation village. For three centuries it was a courthouse and, in 1794, was the site of the first Masonic ceremony in Gloucestershire, but today it's a friendly inn with comfy accommodation and a drying room for walkers' gear – it stands on the Cotswold Way. A great place to rest and refuel, the interconnecting bars and dining areas are full of character with panelled walls, stone, tiled or carpeted floors, and open log fires to relax in front of, on cold winter days. Attractive terrace and courtyard gardens.

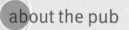

about the pub

The Falcon Inn
New Street, Painswick
Stroud, Gloucestershire GL6 6UN
Tel: 01452 814222
www.falconinn.com

DIRECTIONS: centre of the village, opposite the church

PARKING: 25

OPEN: daily; all day

FOOD: daily; snacks all day

BREWERY/COMPANY: free house

REAL ALE: Hook Norton Bitter & Old Hooky, Wadworth 6X, Greene King IPA

DOGS: welcome in the bar

ROOMS: 12 en suite

Food

At lunchtime expect to find filled paninis, pasta meals, home-made soups, and classic pub favourites – ham, egg and chips, Irish stew and toad-in-the-hole – on the printed or blackboard menus. Evening additions may include seasonal game from local shoots, beef Wellington, calves' liver and bacon, and organic Cockleford trout. Afternoon teas.

Family facilities

The Falcon has a children's licence, so all ages are welcome inside and there's a children's menu, smaller portions of adult dishes, and high chairs.

Alternative refreshment stops

There are several possibilities in Painswick – a pub, a tea room, a couple of restaurants and several shops. There is also a pub in Edge, the Edgemoor Inn, (a few minutes walk off the route).

☛ Where to go from here

Visit Prinknash Abbey at Cranham and learn more about monastic life, then visit the adjacent Bird and Deer Park where children can feed and stroke the fallow deer and see exotic pheasants, peacocks and wildfowl (www.prinknash-bird-and-deerpark.co.uk). Painswick Rococo Garden (www.rococogarden.co.uk) is the only one of its period to survive complete and is a magical experience at any time of the year.

Sherston and Easton Grey

The infant Bristol Avon links attractive stone villages on this pastoral ramble on the fringes of the Cotswolds.

Legend of a local hero

The Bristol Avon is little more than a wide, shallow stream as it flows through the rolling countryside west of Malmesbury. This peaceful river enhances the little stone villages in this unspoilt area. Between Colerne and Malmesbury, 18 villages are officially part of the Cotswold Area of Outstanding Natural Beauty. Sherston must rank among the most attractive, with its wide High Street lined with interesting 17th- and 18th-century buildings. It has been suggested that Sherston is Sceorstan where in 1016 Edmund Ironside won a battle against the Danes led by King Canute. The legend of John Rattlebone, a local yeoman promised land by Ironside in return for service against the Danes, is deep rooted. Sadly, this brave knight was wounded in battle and although he staunched his bleeding with a stone tile and continued fighting, he reputedly died as Canute's army withdrew. Other traditions say Rattlebone survived to claim his reward.

Later traditions tell us that the stone effigy on the south side of the porch of the parish church is that of Rattlebone, and that an ancient timber chest in the church, marked with the initials R B, is where he kept his armour. The Rattlebone Inn keeps his name alive.

Peaceful riverside paths lead you downstream to Easton Grey. Set around a 16th-century stone bridge and climbing a short, curving street is an intimate huddle of ancient stone houses, with mullioned windows, steep roofs and flower-filled gardens along the river bank. Set back on a rise above the river is Easton Grey House, a handsome 18th-century manor, surrounded by elegant gardens and lovely valley views.

the walk

1 On Sherston's High Street, walk towards the village stores, pass The Rattlebone

3h00 · **6.75 MILES** · **10.9 KM** · **LEVEL 1 2 3**

Inn and turn right into **Noble Street**. Pass Grove Road and take the footpath left up a flight of steps. Cross a cul-de-sac and follow a metalled footpath to a gate. Continue at the rear of houses to a further gate.

2 Bear diagonally right across a field to a gate and go forward in a second paddock to a kissing gate onto a lane. Turn right, cross the river and turn left, signed 'Foxley'. At the end of woodland on your left, take the footpath left through a gate. Follow the track across **Pinkney Park** to a gate.

3 Remain on the track, bearing left beside the wall and continuing ahead through a second gate towards **farm buildings**. Where it then curves left, turn right into the farmyard. Cross to join a concrete path in the far right corner and walk on to a stile. Go forward, joining the left-hand boundary, sticking with it in the next field.

4 In the third field, climb right to a gate and then bear half left along the field to a stile at the far side. Over a bridge and further stile, walk on past **game bird pens** and then beside a ranch fence, where there is a view to **Easton Grey House**. Drop through a gate at the far end onto a lane.

5 Turn left into **Easton Grey**. Cross the river and immediately turn right. Approaching entrance gates at the top, go left on a footpath past a **barn** into a gravel yard. Cross to a gate and keep ahead to a stile, just right of the field corner.

MAP: OS Explorer 168 Stroud, Tetbury & Malmesbury

START/FINISH: Sherston High Street; plenty of roadside parking; grid ref: ST 853858

PATHS: field and parkland paths, tracks, metalled lanes, 10 stiles

LANDSCAPE: river valley and gently rolling farmland

PUBLIC TOILETS: none on route

TOURIST INFORMATION: Malmesbury, tel 01666 823748

THE PUB: The Rattlebone Inn, Sherston

Getting to the start

Sherston stands midway between Bath and Cirencester on the B4040, 5 miles (8km) west of Malmesbury. There is parking beside the wide High Street.

Researched and written by:
David Hancock, Dennis Kelsall

Left: The Avon passes through Easton Grey
Right: Sherston church where you will see the effigy of Rattlebone on the south of the porch

Maintain direction across the next field and gently descend to follow a track into the next field.

6 Turn right along the field-edge to the next corner and bear off right downhill through scrub to a **footbridge**. Keep ahead beside a ruin to a gate. Cross a stile and continue at the edge of a field to another stile by a gate. Follow a track downhill through trees to meet the **Fosse Way** beside a bridge. Turn right along the track and continue for 0.5 mile (800m) to a road.

7 Cross straight over and keep to the byway to another road. Bear left, but then keep ahead where the lane veers sharp left. Follow the track for another 0.5 mile (800m), passing a stile and later, the access to **Ladyswood Polo Ground**. Shortly beyond that, leave over a stile hidden in the right-hand hedge. Bear left, crossing to a

what to look for

The wide, hedged and dead-straight track which you follow on your return route to Sherston is the Fosse Way. This is the ancient Roman road which ran from Lincoln to Exeter and is so named because it was bordered on both sides by a 'fosse' or ditch.

small gate in the set-back portion of the opposite hedge, also not obvious. Now head diagonally right across a large paddock, joining a track to a gate.

8 It leads through to a **racecourse training gallop**. Keep ahead, passing left beside the barrier to a gate beyond. Walk through scrub to another gate and follow a track out to a lane. Turn left and continue past a crossroads and then a junction, remaining with the main lane beyond as it winds back into **Sherston**.

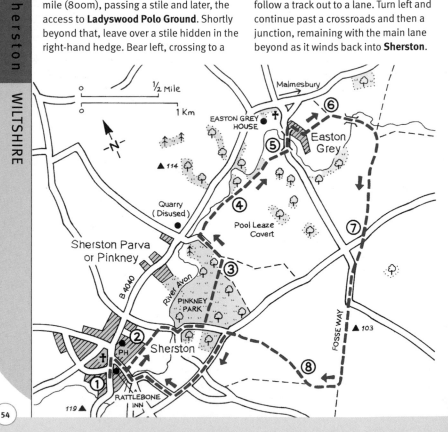

The Rattlebone Inn

This lively 16th-century village inn takes its name from the local hero John Rattlebone who, according to legend, died fighting King Canute in the Battle of Sherston in 1016. Inside, you'll find a rambling series of beamed rooms with old pews and settles, jugs and bottles hanging from the low beams, a mix of sturdy country furnishings, numerous cuttings and memorabilia relating to the pub's long and eventful history, and a good pubby atmosphere. The separate public bar has traditional and modern pub games including alley skittles. The food is good, the handpumped beer from Young's first-class and there's a decent range of wines by the glass. An annual boules championship is held on the Saturday closest to Bastille Day and features 132 teams from across Europe – the largest one-day boules event in the country. Pretty rear garden with flowerbeds, a gravel terrace and, naturally, four boules pitches.

Food

Enjoyable 'rattles snacks' include filled paninis, crusty sandwiches and ploughman's lunches. Regular lunchtime favourites take in smoked haddock fishcakes with leek sauce, home-made beef burger on foccacia bread with salad, and 'rattlebangers' with mash. The separate evening menu is more extensive.

Family facilities

Families are welcome in the pub. There are high chairs for toddlers and children can order small portions of main menu dishes.

Alternative refreshment stops

Sherston's other pub is the Carpenters Arms on the Malmesbury road out of the village.

☛ Where to go from here

Head north into Gloucestershire to visit Westonbirt Arboretum (www.forestry.gov.uk /westonbirt), one of the finest and most important collections of trees and shrubs in the country.

WALK

Sherston · **WILTSHIRE**

about the pub

The Rattlebone Inn
Church Street, Sherston
Malmesbury, Wiltshire SN16 0LR
Tel: 01666 840871

DIRECTIONS: on the High Street, opposite the church

PARKING: use High Street

OPEN: daily; all day

FOOD: daily

BREWERY/COMPANY: Young's Brewery

REAL ALE: Young's Bitter, Special & Triple A, Smiles Best

DOGS: welcome in the public bar only

Malmesbury and the Fosse Way

Visit the splendid remnants of an ancient abbey church and follow in the footsteps of Roman soldiers.

in fine arches, vaulting and tracery, while the early Norman carving in the porch is particularly striking.

An unusual and rare feature is the curious watching loft that projects from the

Malmesbury Abbey

All that is left of Malmesbury's great monastery, founded in 676 by St Aldhelm, is part of the abbey church, which survived Henry VIII's Dissolution only because it was granted to the town for use as its parish church. The building dates from the 12th century and was constructed on a vast cruciform plan. Beside it stood a secluded cloister surrounded by the domestic buildings in which the monks lived.

If what remains is anything to go by, then the medieval building must have been a truly magnificent sight, a long avenue of soaring columns lifting the roof high above the church. Exquisite stonework is revealed

upper wall high above the southern side of the nave; nobody is really sure what purpose it served. Also of interest is the tomb of Alfred the Great's grandson, King Athelstan. He commissioned the first translation of the Bible into English, and his tomb stands near the north west corner of the church, while outside is the grave of Hannah Twynnoy, a servant at the town's White Lion Inn, who died after being mauled by a tiger in 1703.

the ride

1 Out of The Vine Tree car park, pedal easily away along the lane to the left, reaching a junction after 0.75 mile (1.2km).

Keep left with the main lane, before long arriving at **Foxley**. Go right, passing the community's tiny church.

2 Continue along the lane for 2 miles (3.2km) to the outskirts of Malmesbury, where **Common Road** joins from the right. Keep going as the road shortly winds down to cross the Sherston branch of the River Avon, where there is a view right to the **abbey church**. Climb away, remaining with the main road as it bends right to a T-junction. Go right, and then at the next junction, in front of The Triangle and **war memorial,** go right again to the abbey. It is perhaps a good idea to park your bike there while you explore the town centre, just a short walk away.

3 Ride back to the junction by the war memorial and now turn right along Gloucester Road, passing through the town to a mini-roundabout. There, bear left into Park Road, signed to **Park Road Industrial Estate**. Fork off right after 300yds (274m) to remain with Park Road. After passing a few more houses, the route abruptly leaves the town, and continues beside the Avon's **Tetbury Branch** along a narrow hedged lane.

4 Reaching a T-junction, go right, crossing the river towards **Brokenborough**. The lane climbs easily to the village, passing the **Rose and Crown** and then falling to the church and Church Lane. After 100yds (91m), turn off left into a lane marked as a cul-de-sac. After dropping to re-cross the river, the narrow lane climbs past **Brook Farm**, initially steeply, but soon levelling to continue between the fields.

2h00 | **9.75 MILES** | **15.7 KM** | **LEVEL 1 2 3**

MAP: OS Explorer 168 Stroud, Tetbury & Malmesbury

START/FINISH: The Vine Tree, Norton (ask permission first); grid ref: ST 887846

TRAILS/TRACKS: country lanes and gravel tracks, a short town section at Malmesbury

LANDSCAPE: undulating hill farmland

PUBLIC TOILETS: in Malmesbury behind the town square

TOURIST INFORMATION: Malmesbury; tel: 01666 823748

CYCLE HIRE: C H White & Son, 51 High Street, Malmesbury, tel 01666 822330 (prior bookings only) – alternative start

THE PUB: The Vine Tree, Norton

🛈 Great care to be taken through Malmesbury; steep descent and climb at Roman Bridge on the Fosse Way

Getting to the start

Malmesbury stands midway between Chippenham and Cirencester just off the A429 on the B4040. Norton is 3 miles (4.8km) to the south west . On entering the village, turn right, signposted Foxley, follow the road round to the right for the pub.

Why do this cycle ride?

This undemanding ride combines historic Malmesbury with quiet lanes and good off-road cycling. The route roughly follows part of two shallow valleys which converge on Malmesbury. The 'circle' is completed along a straight stretch of the Fosse Way.

Researched and written by: Dennis Kelsall

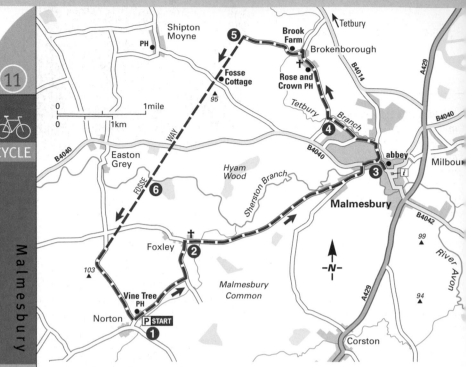

5 The track ends at a T-junction with a broad, straight track, the **Fosse Way**. Go left. Very soon, the tarmac gives way to coarse gravel and stone, and although the way is firm, the surface is loose in places and there is a risk of skidding if you travel at speed. After 0.5 mile (800m), cross a lane by **Fosse Cottage** and carry on past a water-pumping station for another mile (1.6km) to the B4040. Keep an eye open for fast-moving traffic as you cross and continue, the track, before long, starting a steepening descent. It bends at the bottom to a bridge over the **Sherston Branch**.

6 Although widened in modern times the upstream portion of the bridge is original and dates back to a Roman settlement beside the river. The climb away on the far bank is very steep, and you may have to get off and push. Beyond, the way runs easily again for 0.5 mile (800m) to another road crossing. Keep ahead with the byway, the surface now of earth and a little rutted, shortly emerging onto another lane. Go ahead, staying with it as it soon bends left away from the line of the Roman road. Eventually dropping to a T-junction at the edge of **Norton**, go left to The Vine Tree.

The south view of the remnants of Malmesbury Abbey

The Vine Tree

The Vine Tree is a converted 16th-century mill house close to Westonbirt Arboretum, and is well worth seeking out for its interesting modern pub food and memorable outdoor summer dining. The tranquil sun-trap terrace includes a fountain, lavender hedge, pagodas, trailing vines and a barbecue. There's also a 2 acre (0.8ha) garden with a play area, and two boules pitches. If the weather is wet, be consoled with a pint of Fiddlers Elbow by the log fire in the main bar, with its old oak beams and flagstone floors. As well as a changing selection of real ales, there's a carefully selected list of wines (up to 30 by the glass), and decent coffee. Cooking is modern British, everything is made on the premises, and meals are served in the pine-furnished dining areas.

Food

The menu changes daily and closely follows the seasons, using local produce wherever possible. Choose from light bites (smoked haddock kedgeree, roast Cotswold pork baguette) and vegetarian options (wild mushroom and feta risotto) or trio of local award-winning sausages with bubble and squeak and a grain mustard sauce, or gilt-head bream with lemongrass and sweet basil broth. Imaginative puddings.

Family facilities

Well-behaved children are welcome in the pub. High chairs are at hand, a children's menu, including home-made chicken nuggets, is available as are smaller portions, plus colouring equipment to keep youngsters amused. Sun-trap terrace and a huge garden/field with play area and space for impromptu football and cricket.

about the pub

The Vine Tree
Foxley Road, Norton
Malmesbury, Wiltshire SN16 0JP
Tel: 01666 837654
www.thevinetree.co.uk

DIRECTIONS: see Getting to the Start
PARKING: 100
OPEN: daily; all day Sunday
FOOD: daily; all day Sunday (& Saturday if fine) in summer
BREWERY/COMPANY: free house
REAL ALE: Butcombe Bitter, Wychwood Fiddlers Elbow, Hook Norton Bitter, guest beers
ROOMS: 4 en suite

Alternative refreshment stops

Various pubs and cafés in Malmesbury; the Rose & Crown at Brokenborough

☞ Where to go from here

Visit the impressive remains of Malmesbury's Benedictine abbey, and in the spring and summer visit the Abbey House Gardens (www.abbeyhousegardens. co.uk). In nearby Tetbury the Police Museum (www.tetbury.org) explains how policing was carried out in the early 1900s.

Corsham and Corsham Park

Explore this architectural treasure of a town and the adjacent Corsham Park.

Architectural delights

Bath stone characterises this handsome little market town. An air of prosperity pervades the streets where the 15th-century Flemish gabled cottages and baroque-pedimented 17th-century Hungerford Almshouses mix with larger Georgian residences. Architectural historian Nikolaus Pevsner wrote: 'Corsham has no match in Wiltshire for the wealth of good houses'.

Spend time exploring the heart of the town as many of the fine stone buildings along the High Street, Church Street and Priory Street have been well preserved. The Heritage Centre in the High Street has lively exhibits. The Town Hall was formerly the market hall with one storey and open arches before conversion in 1882. North of the post office the unspoiled line of 17th-century weavers' cottages are known as the Flemish Buildings. This was the centre of the cloth industry where the Flemish weavers settled following religious persecution in their homeland. In Church Street, note the gabled cottages of the 18th-

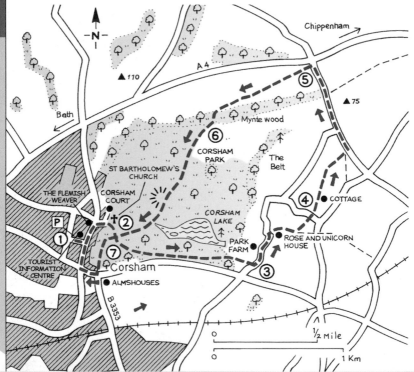

century weavers, with their ornate porches and a door on the first floor for taking in the raw wool.

The finest of the houses is Corsham Court, a splendid Elizabethan mansion built in 1582. It was bought in 1745 by Paul Methuen to house the family's collection of 16th- and 17th-century Italian and Flemish Master paintings and statuary. The house and park you see today are principally the work of 'Capability' Brown, John Nash and Thomas Bellamy. Do take a tour of the house. You will see the outstanding collection of over 140 paintings, including pictures by Rubens, Turner, Reynolds and Van Dyck, fine statuary and bronzes, and the famous collection of English furniture, notably pieces by Robert Adam and Thomas Chippendale.

the walk

1 Turn left out of the long stay car park, then left again along Post Office Lane to reach the High Street. Turn left, pass the **tourist information centre** and turn right into Church Street opposite The Flemish Weaver. Pass the impressive entrance to Corsham Court and enter **St Bartholomew's churchyard.**

2 Bear right across the churchyard, leaving through a gate and walk ahead to join the main path across **Corsham Park**. Turn left and walk along the south side of the park, passing **Corsham Lake**, to reach a stile and gate. Keep ahead to follow a fenced path beside a track to a kissing gate and proceed across a field to a stile and lane.

Eighteenth-century houses on Corsham High Street

1h45 · 4 MILES · 6.4 KM · LEVEL 1 2 3

MAP: OS Explorer 156 Chippenham & Bradford on Avon
START/FINISH: Corsham: long stay car park in Newlands Lane; grid ref: ST 871704
PATHS: field paths and country lanes, 10 stiles
LANDSCAPE: town streets, gently undulating parkland, farmland
PUBLIC TOILETS: short stay car park by shopping precinct
TOURIST INFORMATION: Corsham, tel 01249 714660
THE PUB: The Flemish Weaver, Corsham
🅛 An easy walk although care should be taken along the road section

Getting to the start

Corsham is just 4 miles (6.4km) south west of Chippenham, where the B3353 meets the A4. The walk begins from the town's long stay car park on Newland's Road, signposted from the main road.

Researched and written by:
David Hancock, Dennis Kelsall

*Corsham Court, framed by an arched gateway,
is filled with fine artwork and furniture*

5 Go through the gate in the wall on your left and walk along the centre of parkland pasture. Through a metal kissing gate, maintain your direction, gradually closing with the left boundary to reach another kissing gate on the edge of **Myrtle Wood**. Follow the wide path to a further gate and bear half right to a stile.

6 Keep the same direction on a vague trod across the parkland beyond, joining the far boundary and following it left to a kissing gate hidden in a thicket in the corner. Continue by the perimeter to a further gate in the next corner, where there are fine views right to **Corsham Court**. Follow the field-edge as it bends right, but when it then curves right again, keep ahead to join the churchyard wall. Pass the stile by which you entered the park to another stile ahead.

7 Turn left down an avenue of trees to emerge onto Lacock Road, noting the **stone almshouses** opposite. Turn right, and then go right again along the pedestrianised High Street. Turn left back along Post Office Lane to the **car park**.

3 Turn left, pass **Park Farm**, a splendid stone farmhouse on your left, and shortly take the waymarked footpath right along a drive to pass **Rose and Unicorn House**. At its end on the right, cross a stile and follow the right-hand field-edge to a stile, then bear half left to a stone stile in the field corner. Ignore the path arrowed right and head straight across the field to a further stile and **metalled farm track**.

4 Through a gap diagonally opposite, bear half left to a stone stile to the left of a **cottage**. Maintain direction across the next field and pass through a gap in the far left corner. Continue along the left-hand side of a field to a stile in the corner. Turn left along the lane for 0.5 mile (800m) to the A4.

what to look for

Note the Folly along Church Street, an artificial ruin, set with church windows, built by Nash in 1800 to hide Ethelred House from Corsham Court. Seek out the grave of Sarah Jarvis behind St Bartholomew's Church; she died in 1703 aged 107 having grown a new set of teeth! Look for the plaque at 38 High Street informing you that Sir Michael Tippett, one of Britain's greatest 20th-century composers, lived there between 1960 and 1970.

The Flemish Weaver

Formerly a run-down drinking pub called the Pack Horse, the fortunes of this beautifully positioned town pub, opposite a charming row of old weavers' cottages, have recently been restored. The name refers to the Flemish weavers brought over to the town to help establish the wool trade. The atmosphere is now more continental bistro than town centre pub, with a bright and cheerful interior and pavement seating. You can relax and enjoy quality real ales, good wines by the glass, and freshly prepared food using local and organic produce. Add efficient and very helpful staff and a warm welcome to children and you have a great post-walk refreshment stop.

Food
For lunch, order filled baguettes, ploughman's lunches or, perhaps, ham, egg and chips, spaghetti with stir-fried vegetables, or braised steak and vegetables from the daily menu. Evening additions may take in organic rump steak with peppercorn sauce and pan-fried tuna with oriental sauce.

Family facilities
Although there are no special facilities children of all ages are made to feel very welcome. Smaller portions of adult dishes are readily available and there's a safe garden that families can use on sunny days.

Alternative refreshment stops
Corsham is well served by pubs, cafés and restaurants.

☛ Where to go from here
Visit Sheldon Manor (3 miles/4.7km north), Wiltshire's oldest inhabited manor house. Dating from 1282, this well-preserved Plantaganet house features a 15th-century chapel, authentic furnishings and beautiful informal terraced gardens. Near by is the preserved National Trust village of Lacock with its fine abbey and photography museum (www.nationaltrust.org.uk).

about the pub

The Flemish Weaver
63 High Street, Corsham
Wiltshire SN13 0EZ
Tel: 01249 701929

DIRECTIONS: on High Street next to the Town Hall

PARKING: use town car parks

OPEN: daily

FOOD: no food Tuesday & Sunday evenings

BREWERY/COMPANY: Unique Pub Company

REAL ALE: Banks's Original, Moles Best, 2 guest beers

DOGS: allowed in the garden only

Between Holt and Lacock

Gardens, a 15th-century house and a former abbey are highlights that await discovery on this ride.

Two great manors

Holt's lovely gardens, surrounding an 18th-century house, were laid out in the early 1900s by Sir George Hastings, who set out to combine formal composition with corners of natural beauty. The house, which is not open to the public, is built upon a former textile mill, and is known as 'The Courts', for it was here that disputes were once brought for settlement.

Constructed in 1480 by Thomas Tropnell on the site of an earlier fortified manor, from which the moat and defensive foundations survive, Great Chalfield is a wonderful example of the architecture of its period, when comfort and decoration were assuming precedence over the Spartan necessities of protection. In creating his manor house, Tropnell also made alterations to the adjacent church,

adding a chapel on its south side. It is entered through a finely carved stone screen portraying the heraldry of the Tropnell family. Another interesting feature is a three-decker pulpit, above which is a wooden canopy, a sounding board to project the speaker's voice.

Both properties belong to the National Trust, as does Lacock Abbey (see also Route 15).

the ride

1 From the car park, go to the main street and follow it right, shortly turning right again into **Leigh Road** opposite The Tollgate Inn. The way is signed to Great Chalfield. After less than 0.5 mile (800m), fork off right onto a lesser lane, passing through the parkland surrounding **Holt Manor**. At the end turn right yet again, the lane eventually winding around to **Great Chalfield Manor**.

2 Swing right opposite the entrance, joining a gently rising avenue that before long leads to a T-junction. To shorten the ride, go left and at the crossroads, go left again to pick up the return instructions at Point 7. Otherwise, turn right to reach **Broughton Gifford**. Carry on, passing **The Bell** at the far side of the village to then fork left towards Melksham. After 0.33 mile (500m), go left beside a cottage into **Norrington Lane**. At its eventual end go right along the A365, dropping to traffic lights by **Shaw church**. Turn left along the B3353 towards Corsham and keep going to leave

Left: Great Chalfield church beyond a pond

Whitley behind, until you arrive at a turning off on the right, where the road bends left.

3 At this point you have a choice, and can cut off a corner by following a bridlepath. However, after rain the way can be muddy, and its uneven nature may render it unsuitable for very young or inexperienced riders. The alternative is to carry on along the road to **Gastard** and turn right into Lanes End opposite the **Harp and Crown**. Follow it out of the village, continuing past lesser lanes on the left, eventually arriving at the point at which the short cut joins from the right.

For the short cut, turn right along Westlands Lane, and after the houses finish, look for adjacent gates on the left, almost opposite **farm buildings**. Pass through the rightmost one of the two and follow the left-hand field-edge to the corner. Through another gate a grassy path drops into trees, continuing as a narrow hedged way. It soon widens and later, by **Catridge Farm**, joins a tarmac drive, which at its far end meets a lane. Go right.

4 Follow the lane to the A350. Dismount and cross with care to a gap in the opposite hedge. Continue along a short street to a mini-roundabout at the edge of Lacock. Bear left into the village, then turn right to **Lacock Abbey** and **The Red Lion**.

5 Return to the main street and turn right, passing **The George Inn** to leave the village and meet the A350 once more at traffic lights, which enable you to cross. Go right and then immediately left towards **Notton**. Stay with the main lane for 2 miles (3.2km), crossing a couple of railway

| 3h30 | 10 MILES | 28.1 KM | LEVEL 1 2 3 |

SHORTER ALTERNATIVE ROUTE

| 1h30 | 6.25 MILES | 17.5 KM | LEVEL 1 2 3 |

MAP: OS Explorer 156 Chippenham & Bradford-on-Avon

START/FINISH: Car park in Holt; grid ref: ST 861619

TRAILS/TRACKS: lanes and quiet roads, short section on a main road, one off-road section that can be avoided

LANDSCAPE: low-lying hills bordering the Avon valley

PUBLIC TOILETS: at car park opposite the entrance to The Courts Garden

TOURIST INFORMATION: Melksham, tel 01225 707424

CYCLE HIRE: none locally

THE PUB: The Red Lion, Lacock

🔴 Care crossing main road at Lacock; initial section of bridleway cut-through may be difficult after wet weather, or for inexperienced riders.

Getting to the start
Holt lies between Melksham and Bradford-on-Avon on the B3107.

Why do this cycle ride?
Although a long ride, the hills are gentle and there is easy cycling and much to see. The circuit begins at Holt, whilst only a couple of miles (3.2km) away is a charming 15th-century house. As you return the route passes through Lacock. A much shorter ride is possible linking Holt and Great Chalfield.

Researched and written by: Dennis Kelsall

bridges. Shortly after the second bridge, take the first turning off left, **Ladbrook Lane**, signed to Neston. It drops past the cemetery then re-crosses the railway, rising beyond and eventually reaching a crossroads.

6 Straight over, continue climbing past **Monk's Park**, at the top, turning sharp right to **Neston**. Keep ahead until you reach a fork and there bear left. Steadily losing height,

carry on towards **Atworth**. Where the lane ends at the A365, go left and then almost immediately right, bearing left with the main lane as you leave the village towards **Stonar**. The shorter route rejoins from the left at a minor crossroads after 0.75 mile (1.2km).

7 Keep ahead to a fork and bear left, following the lane all the way back to Holt. Turn left in front of **The Tollgate Inn** to return through the village to the car park.

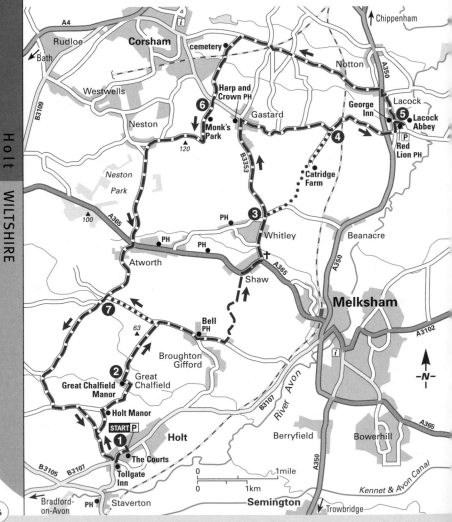

The Red Lion

Set in the centre of this famous National Trust village, immortalised in many a TV and film recording, the Red Lion is a tall, imposing red-brick Georgian coaching inn that has managed to retain its traditional character despite the crowds of tourists. Inside the three rambling, interconnecting bars there is plenty to catch the eye, from the old beams and the crackling log fires to the collections of farming implements, old oil paintings and the sturdy old furnishings on rug-strewn flagstone and bare board floors. A great place to relax after exploring the village, with excellent Wadworth ales on tap, and a sheltered, gravelled rear courtyard garden with abundant shrubs, flowers and picnic benches. Comfortable accommodation in period furnished bedrooms.

Food

Good bar food ranges from traditional snacks such as home-made soup and bread, decent ploughman's lunches and sandwiches on a printed menu to daily blackboard specials, perhaps steak and kidney pie, venison steak with red wine sauce, and lamb and apricot casserole.

Family facilities

Families are made very welcome, the rambling interior having plenty of secluded areas for children. There's a separate menu for younger children and smaller portions of adult dishes are available.

Alternative refreshment stops

In Holt you have the choice of the Old Ham Tree or the Tollgate Inn (children over 10 only). There are tea rooms and The George Inn (see Route 15, page 75) in Lacock. Along the way are the Bell at Broughton Gifford and the Harp and Crown in Gastard.

about the pub

The Red Lion
High Street, Lacock
Chippenham, Wiltshire SN15 2LQ
Tel: 01249 730456

DIRECTIONS: situated opposite the entrance to Lacock Abbey in the village centre

PARKING: 70

OPEN: daily

FOOD: daily

BREWERY/COMPANY: Wadworth Brewery

REAL ALE: Wadworth 6X, Henry's IPA, JCB and seasonal beers

ROOMS: 6 en suite

☞ Where to go from here

Explore the attractive gardens at The Courts in Holt and make time to visit the enchanting Great Chalfield Manor, one of the most perfect examples of the late medieval English manor house. Lacock Abbey and the Fox Talbot Museum (photography) are also worth visiting. The National Trust's website (www.nationaltrust.org.uk) has information about all these attractions.

A circuit from Bisley

From beautiful Bisley, this ramble follows undulating field paths taking in small villages along the way.

Beautiful Bisley

One of the loveliest Cotwold villages, Bisley is known for its well-dressing ceremony on Ascension Day, a tradition dating from the restoration of the wells in Wells Street in 1863 by the vicar, Thomas Keble.

Moss and flowers are collected to cover the frames and hoops carried in procession to the wells by 22 children from the local Bluecoat school.

On Ascension Day, a service is held in the church, then the children's procession forms; the oldest children carry the largest floral stars at the front. Led by the band and the vicar, the procession marches down to the wells where the vicar performs a short blessing. The flowers are arranged by the children to spell 'Ascension' and 'AD' and the current year, whilst garlands, floral hoops, and Stars of David are laid about the wells. A hymn is sung and the children have tea followed by village sports, such as egg-and-spoon and sack races.

Bisley is remarkable in a number of ways. In the churchyard is a 13th-century Poor Soul's Light, the only outdoor example in the country. It was used to light Mass candles on behalf of those who were too poor to buy their own. And then there is the Bisley Boy. Legend says that the real Queen Elizabeth I is buried in Bisley churchyard. During a visit as a girl, apparently, she fell and died. A local boy who closely resembled her took her place and went on to become queen.

the walk

1 Walk down the hill from the Bear Inn to the **post office** and turn right. Keep left with the main street past a fork. As it climbs away, take the first turn left to a crossroads with the main road. Go ahead towards Waterlane and Sapperton, remaining with the lane as it turns abruptly right at a junction.

2 After 0.25 mile (400m), just past **Rectory Farm**, turn through a gate on the right and follow a track at the field-edge. Emerging beside a road junction, cross to a stile opposite and walk on to another stile in the far corner of a paddock. Setting a course slightly right of ahead, strike across the next three fields, passing through a gap to continue at the edge of the fourth field. Nearing the corner, slip through another gap and turn left. Keep going beyond the hedge end to the opposite corner. Over a stile, bear left on a line past **three spaced trees** to the top of a wooded bank. Drop to another field, there go half right, crossing a track to a stile at the bottom. Follow a path behind houses, turning left between the gardens to emerge onto a lane in **Bournes Green**.

MAP: OS Explorer 168 Stroud, Tetbury & Malmesbury

START/FINISH: In Bisley village near the Bear Inn; grid ref: SO 903060

PATHS: tracks, fields, lanes, 20 stiles

LANDSCAPE: secluded valleys, villages, open wold

PUBLIC TOILETS: none on route

TOURIST INFORMATION: Stroud, tel 01453 760960

THE PUB: Bear Inn, Bisley

Getting to the start

Served only by country lanes, Bisley is 3.5 miles (5.6km) east of Stroud above the head of the Toadsmoor valley. Park below the Bear Inn in George Street, which although bearing no name plate, runs north of the church from the pub down to the post office.

Researched and written by:
Dennis Kelsall, Christopher Knowles

Some of The Seven Springs at Bisley

3 Go right and then left to another junction, there descending the grass bank ahead to follow the lane below out of the hamlet. Rising steeply beyond a dip, the lane later bends sharp left. Leave over a stile by a gate on the right. Immediately, climb left up a wooded bank and continue across a clearing to a double stile. Strike diagonally across the fields, leaving onto a lane at the edge of **Oakridge Lynch**. Over a stile opposite, cross a further field to reach another lane.

4 Walk right as far as a crossroads, then turn left, signed to **Frampton Mansell**. Just beyond a green where the **old water pump** serves as a war memorial, take the second of two lanes off left. Stay with the main lane, forking right and joining a wider lane to Daneway and Cirencester.

5 Approaching Far Oakridge, turn left onto a track which leads to **Waterlane**. At the junction, take the second of the two lanes on the right, signed to **Bisley** and **Stroud**, then at the next crossroads choose the leftmost of two lanes before you. Follow it down to a **farm** and keep left on a track. Where that eventually splits bear left to a **gate** facing you at the bottom.

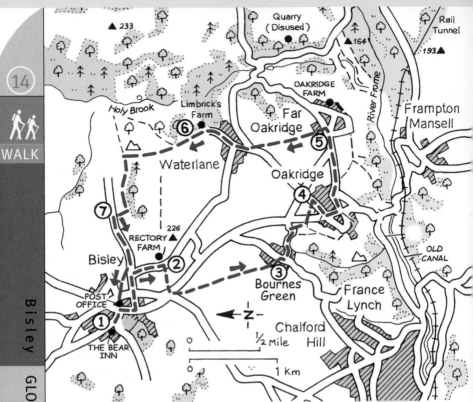

6 Climb straight up the bank in front, continuing forward across a field to a wood. Keep ahead, dropping through the trees and across a field beyond before turning left to rise along the base of a shallow valley. Carry on from field to field, shortly passing a couple of **ponds**. About 100yds (91m) above them, go right, cross a stream and skirt the field-edge below trees. Climb to a stile in the top corner to reach **Heyhedge Lane**.

7 Follow it left to a junction, leaving just beyond onto a track on the right. Where that swings right keep ahead to a kissing gate, crossing a field to another gate. Emerging onto a lane at the edge of **Bisley**, go left and immediately left again on a contained path that terminates abruptly onto a street. Cross to another path opposite that ends near the **post office**. Go left and right back to the Bear Inn.

what to look for

In Bisley look for the impressive building which houses the famous well. The structure, restored by Thomas Keble, is a semicircular stone building and the water pours out of five Gothic-arched recesses into a shallow stone trough. Water also emanates from channels at either side, into deeper troughs before flowing away underground.

Bear Inn

A former courthouse built in the 16th century, the Bear opened as a village inn around 1766. Its outstanding features include a huge inglenook fireplace, a bread oven and an old priest hole; though the rock-hewn cellars including a well are more likely Tudor. The super front bar has a relaxed atmosphere, old oak settles, a few scrubbed tables on polished flagstones, and a huge inglenook fireplace that dominates the room. Locals and walkers congregate here quaffing pints of Pedigree, while diners head for the stone-walled dining area for good home-made bar food. When the sun shines, the sheltered flagstoned courtyard or the small, shaded garden across the road are the places to sit and enjoy this attractive, mellow stone village.

Bisley

Food

You will find a good range of 'bear burgers', 'bear baguettes' (lamb with redcurrant jelly), 'bear necessities' (sautéed potato and onions with sausage and mustard) and 'bear essentials' which include rabbit and vegetable pie, casserole of prawns and white fish in cider. Blackboard specials and home-made puddings.

Family facilities

Children are welcome in the family area. No children's menu but smaller portions (Bear Cubs Food) of adult dishes are available.

Alternative refreshment stops

In Oakridge the Butcher's Arms is on the walk whilst there is another pub in Bisley, the Stirrup Cup, which serves food along with Hook Norton and Wadworth ales.

☛ Where to go from here

Cirencester is of interest: at the Corinium Museum (www.cotswold.gov.uk) in Park Street discover the archaeology of the area and one of the finest collections of objects from Roman and Anglo-Saxon Britain.

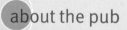

Bear Inn

George Street, Bisley
Stroud, Gloucestershire GL6 7BD
Tel: 01452 770265

DIRECTIONS:	see Getting to the Start
PARKING:	30
OPEN:	daily
FOOD:	no food Sunday evening
BREWERY/COMPANY:	Punch Taverns
REAL ALE:	Tetley, Flowers Original, Charles Wells Bombardier, Marston's Pedigree
DOGS:	welcome inside the pub
ROOMS:	2 bedrooms

A walk around Lacock

Combine a stroll around England's finest medieval village with a riverside walk and a visit to Lacock Abbey, home of photographic pioneer Fox Talbot.

National Trust treasure

Timeless Lacock could be the pattern of the perfect English village with its twisting streets, packed with attractive buildings from the 15th to 18th centuries, possessing all the atmosphere of medieval England.

Half-timbering, lichen grey stone, red-brick and whitewashed façades crowd together. With the founding of an abbey in the 13th

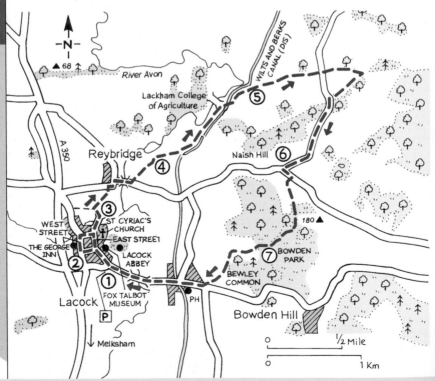

2h45 — **5.75 MILES** — **9.3 KM** — **LEVEL 123**

WALK

Lacock

WILTSHIRE

century, the village grew rich on the wool industry until the mid-18th century when, as an estate-owned village, time seemed to stand still for nearly 100 years.

Lacock Abbey, the village's most beautiful building, began as an Augustinian nunnery in 1232. After the Reformation a Tudor mansion was built on the remains. The abbey passed to the Talbot family through marriage and they Gothicised the south elevation and added the oriel windows. Surrounded by peaceful water-meadows bordering the Avon, this was the setting for the experiments of William Henry Fox Talbot (1800–77), which in 1835 led to the creation of the world's first photographic negative. You can see some of Fox Talbot's work and equipment, alongside photographic exhibitions, in the restored 16th-century barn at the gates.

Architectural gems in Lacock include the timber-framed Sign of the Angel Inn on Church Street, which retains its medieval layout, a 16th-century doorway and the passage through which horses would pass. Near by, Cruck House, with one of its cruck beams exposed, is a rare example of this 14th-century building method.

In West Street, The George Inn dates back to 1361 (see page 75). Next door to the pub take a look at the bus shelter; it was formerly the village smithy. On the corner of East Street is the magnificent 14th-century tithe barn used to store the rents-in-kind paid to the abbey, such as corn, hides and fleeces. The building later became the market hall. Finally, don't miss the 18th-century domed lock-up next door. This is known as a 'blind house', since many of its overnight prisoners were drunks.

MAP: OS Explorer 156 Chippenham & Bradford-on-Avon

START/FINISH: Lacock: Free car park on edge of Lacock; grid ref: ST 918681

PATHS: field paths and tracks; some road walking, 24 stiles

LANDSCAPE: river valley, wooded hillside and parkland

PUBLIC TOILETS: adjacent to Stables Tea Room in Lacock village

TOURIST INFORMATION: Chippenham, tel 01249 706333

THE PUB: The George Inn, Lacock

Getting to the start

Lacock is just off the A350 road, 3.5 miles (5.6km) south of Chippenham. Turn into the village and follow signs for the car park, at its southern end.

Researched and written by:
David Hancock, Dennis Kelsall

the walk

1 The walk begins with a tour of the attractive village. From the car park, cross the road and follow the path into Lacock, passing the entrance to the **abbey**. Turn right into **East Street** opposite The Red Lion and walk down to Church Street. Turn left, then keep left into West Street and go left again into High Street.

2 Having seen the village walk back down East Street. Turn right along **Church Street** and then left in front of the church to cross a bridge over the Bide Brook. Follow the path by the stream then up the lane to the end of the road.

3 Go through the kissing gate on your right and follow the tarmac path across the field to a gate. Pass **cottages** to a lane, turn right, and then right again to cross the **River Avon**. Just beyond, climb the stile on your left. Bear diagonally right across the field to a stile and cross the lane and stile opposite. Follow the path to two squeeze stiles and turn left around the field edge.

4 Half way along the long side, climb two stiles on your left and turn right along the field-edge. Continue around the top end, where a path develops leading into scrub. Over a stile, proceed ahead on a tarmac path beside the old **Wilts and Berks Canal**. Pass an old accommodation bridge and go through a gate into **woodland**. Emerging through another gate into more open ground keep on to a third gate. Immediately before it, climb a stile on the right. Go left across the corner to another stile, from which a **waymarked path** winds up through scrub into a field at the top.

5 Bearing slightly right, proceed across on a trod, joining the left boundary past a jutting corner to a gate. Keep going in the subsequent field to another gate, then

what to look for

Look for the print of Fox Talbot's first photographic negative, showing the abbey's oriel window, beside the window in the south gallery. Explore the cloister court and see where many scenes from Harry Potter and the Philosopher's Stone (2001) were filmed.

follow the left edge to cross a **metalled farm drive**. Now head right to the top corner and cross a stile into the next field. Walk on, bearing round right to another stile by a gate and climb towards a **house** above the far top corner. However, approaching a gate there, double back sharp right below the top edge of the field, passing a second house. Keep ahead, a developing trod guiding you to double stiles. Walk on, describing a left curve to join a metalled farm track that climbs through a gate into **woodland**. Continue beyond to a lane.

6 Turn left, then cross the stile on the right before a house. Follow the left-hand field-edge for 50yds (46m), cross a stile and bear diagonally left to a stile in the field corner. Go left to another stile into woodland and continue through the trees. Proceed ahead along the field-edge beyond to a stile on your right near the next corner. Bear half left across **Bowden Park**, keeping to the left of a **clump of trees**, then bear right and join the bottom boundary as it drops to a stile beside a gate.

7 Head downhill to a stile and turn left with the field-edge, following it around and down to a stile and gate near a house. Walk through to its drive and follow it left. As tarmac gives way to gravel at the bottom of a dip, bear off right across **Bewley Common**, crossing another drive to emerge onto a lane at a junction. Turn right and return to Lacock, where you will find **The George Inn** on West Street.

The George Inn

Steeped in history and much used as a film and television location, this beautiful National Trust village includes an atmospheric inn. Starting life in 1361 as the Black Boy with its own brewery in farm buildings to the rear, its modernisations have preserved and reused many of the original timbers. Central to the bar is a unique mounted dog-wheel built into the open fireplace and used for spit-roasting in the 16th century (the dog was trained to rotate the wheel). Elsewhere in the low-beamed and split-level bar you will find flagstone floors, stone-mullioned windows, candles on close-packed tables, several relaxing armchairs, a few cosy corners, and a log fire in the medieval fireplace. The large and safe garden stretches out on both sides of the rear car park.

Food

In addition to sandwiches, filled baguettes, salads and ploughman's there's a selection of tasty pies, and favourites such as chicken and wild mushrooms in red wine, pork fillet medallions with a Stilton and port sauce, and rack of lamb with orange and mint sauce.

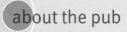

about the pub

The George Inn
4 West Street, Lacock
Chippenham, Wiltshire SN15 2LH
Tel: 01249 730263

DIRECTIONS: See Getting to the start
PARKING: 40
OPEN: daily; all day Saturday & Sunday
FOOD: daily
BREWERY/COMPANY: Wadworth Brewery
REAL ALE: Wadworth 6X, Henry's IPA & JCB
DOGS: welcome in the bar area and garden only

Family facilities

You'll find a warm welcome for children here. There's a children's menu, smaller portions of some main menu dishes, and high chairs are available. Children with some energy left will enjoy the play area in the garden.

Alternative refreshment stops

You are spoiled for choice in Lacock. For snacks and lunches head for the National Trust's Stable Tea Rooms or King John's Hunting Lodge; for pub lunches also try The Red Lion (see Route 13, page 67), or the Carpenters Arms. For something special try the Sign of the Angel restaurant.

☛ Where to go from here

At Lackham Country Park (north of Lacock), historic barns and granaries house an intriguing range of displays depicting Wiltshire agriculture and rural life. There are also walled gardens and a farm park. The Robert Adam-designed Bowood House overlooks terraced gardens and beautiful parkland (www.bowood.org).

From Sapperton to Oakridge

Sapperton was both the focus of a major engineering project and a cradle for cultural change.

Thames and Severn Canal

Sapperton was at the centre of both the Industrial Revolution and the Romantic Revival. In the first case, it was canal technology that came to Sapperton. The Thames and Severn Canal opened in 1789, linking the Thames at Lechlade with the Stroudwater Navigation at Stroud. The Sapperton Tunnel, at 3,400yds (3,109m) long, is one of the longest transport tunnels in the country. The canal was not a success: rock falls and leakages needed constant attention; either there was too much or too little water. The canal closed in 1911.

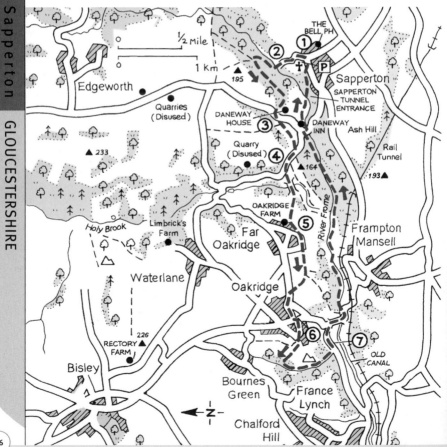

| 3h15 | 6.25 MILES | 10.1 KM | LEVEL 1 2 3 |

It isn't just the great canal tunnel that is of interest in Sapperton. Some of the cottages here were built by disciples of William Morris (1834–96) the doyen of the Arts and Crafts Movement. It aspired to reintroduce to English life a simple yet decorative functionality, in part as a reaction to the mass-production engendered by the Industrial Revolution.

You'll find the finest example of the Arts and Crafts vernacular-style architecture in Sapperton's Upper Dorval House. The entrance to the western end of the Sapperton Tunnel is in fact in the hamlet of Daneway, a short walk along the path from the Daneway Inn, which was formerly called the Bricklayer's Arms. Daneway House, the 14th-century house that was let to followers of William Morris by Earl Bathurst, is a short distance up the road from the pub.

MAP: OS Explorer 168 Stroud, Tetbury & Malmesbury
START/FINISH: Sapperton: park in the village near church; grid ref: SO 947033
PATHS: woodland paths and tracks, fields, lanes and canalside paths, 16 stiles
LANDSCAPE: secluded valleys and villages
PUBLIC TOILETS: none on route
TOURIST INFORMATION: Cirencester, tel 01285 654180
THE PUB: The Bell at Sapperton, Sapperton

Getting to the start

Sapperton lies some 7 miles (11.3km) west of Stroud and is signposted off the A419 to Cirencester. You will find roadside parking at the start of the walk in a cul-de-sac beside the church.

Researched and written by:
Dennis Kelsall, Christopher Knowles

the walk

1 Follow a cul-de-sac from the main lane beside the church, which falls steeply into

the Frome valley. At the entrance to a house at the bottom, bear left on a footpath that drops into trees, crossing the infant river.

2 Climb away on a prominent path through the wood, keeping left where it later forks. When you eventually reach a crossing track, turn left and follow it for 0.5 mile (800m), undulating gently downwards to a lane.

3 Go left and then immediately right over a stile, opposite the entrance to **Daneway House**. Ignore the fenced path and instead pass into the field below it. Walk away along its length on a faint grass track. Emerging onto a lane at the far end, follow it right over a hill, leaving after 250yds (229m) onto a track off left to **Spring Bank House**, not the adjacent path into Siccaridge Wood.

4 After 50yds (46m) and before reaching the house, leave through a **waymarked gap** in the left-hand hedge. To the right, a narrow path follows the edge of a gully down the hill. Passing through a gate lower down, continue at the edge of a small field then go left at the bottom to a stile and slab bridge. Strike across a meadow to a stile and gate, climbing into woodland beyond. Emerging into a field at the top, head half right and carry on through a gap across the next field to a gate below **Oakridge Farm**. A grass track leads out to a lane.

5 Turn left, drop past a junction to Trillis but at a sharp right corner go ahead into a field. Walk to a stile on the far side and cross the next field to a stile and gate in the top right corner. Carry on by the left-hand hedge finally leaving onto a lane. Descend left to into **Oakridge**.

6 Walk past a junction and bear right at a fork, keeping ahead again at a cross-roads to reach the **village green** beyond the school. Carry on past the church to the far end to find a stile between the last two cottages on the right. Behind the cottage go left and over another stile, follow the field-edge down. Approaching the end, cross left and then turn right, striking a diagonal beyond the end of the hedge to the bottom-right corner. Entering **Strawberry Banks Nature Reserve**, take a falling path to the right, emerging below the trees to descend across a superb flower-rich meadow. At the bottom, double back left to follow a path at the base of the valley. Beyond a second meadow, pass into **Three Groves Wood**, and keep going to a lane.

7 Turn left then, at a junction, go right across a bridge. After rounding a bend, leave almost immediately over a footbridge on the left to join the **Thames and Severn Canal tow path**. Walk right, later re-crossing to a lock-side cottage. Briefly follow a track left to a kissing gate through which the path continues beside the old waterway. Eventually the route swaps banks again, before emerging onto a lane by the **Daneway Inn**. Cross the bridge to regain the tow path , which continues for a further 0.33 mile (500m) before ending abruptly at the **Sapperton Tunnel**. Climb around the entrance, into a field and bear half right up to a gate. Walk out to a lane. Go left to its end and then turn right through the churchyard. **The Bell at Sapperton** lies just up the hill.

what to look for

Emerging on the road after Oakridge Farm you are at the edge of the hamlet of Far Oakridge. Painter William Rothenstein lived at Iles Farm between 1913 and 1920, hosting the poets Rabindranath Tagore and W H Davies. Writer and caricaturist Max Beerbohm resided at nearby Winstons Cottage, as did, later, the poet John Drinkwater.

The Bell at Sapperton

Both a local pub and a fine dining venue, the 300-year-old Bell is elegant in an understated way and appeals equally to the business person and the hiker. Standing on the edge of Cirencester Park in classic Cotswold walking country, the stone-built Bell was just another run-down village drinking pub until it was stylishly refurbished in 2000. Expect three cosy, interconnecting dining areas radiating round the central bar, all stone walls, bare boards or polished flagstone floors, open log fires, and tasteful touches such as wine prints on the walls, fresh flowers on scrubbed tables, and newspapers. Yes, innovative modern menus and fine wines attract discerning diners, but The Bell has not forgotten its roots, as there's cracking local ale and scrumpy farm ciders on tap, plus a walkers' snack menu.

Food

Local or organic produce is a feature of the monthly changing menus and daily specials board which highlight fresh Cornish fish. Tuck into an excellent West Country cheese ploughman's with home-made chutney, select a starter of Portland crab risotto or baked goat's cheese with thyme and spiced fig, or opt for something more adventurous, perhaps pan-fried breast of pigeon with black pudding and apples, or free-range chicken breast with potato, butternut and chorizo broth. Chocolate and brandy mousse with Cointreau oranges makes a fitting ending.

Family facilities

Children are allowed in the eating area at lunchtime; over 10s in the evening.

Splendid terraced front garden and rear courtyard seating for fine days.

Alternative refreshment stops

There is a pub in every village you walk through here. In Oakridge the Butcher's Arms requires only a short diversion. In Daneway, the Daneway Inn is on your route.

☛ Where to go from here

Cirencester is not far away. As well as the Corinium Museum (www.cotswolds.gov.uk) and the largest parish church in England, you can explore Cirencester Park. This fine estate, partly designed by poet Alexander Pope, can be accessed from Sapperton.

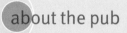

about the pub

The Bell at Sapperton

Sapperton, Cirencester
Gloucestershire GL7 6LE
Tel: 01285 760298
www.foodatthebell.co.uk

DIRECTIONS: The Bell is just up the hill from the church	
PARKING: 60	
OPEN: daily	
FOOD: daily	
BREWERY/COMPANY: free house	
REAL ALE: Uley Old Spot, Goffs Jouster, Wickwar Cotswold Way, Hook Norton Bitter	
DOGS: welcome in the pub	

Around Sapperton

CYCLE

Above the valley
of the River Frome
and through the
Earl of Bathurst's
estate.

Sapperton

GLOUCESTERSHIRE

Sapperton church

There are few churches
dedicated to St Kenelm,
an historical figure
and mentioned in *The
Canterbury Tales*, but
Sapperton's is one. Heir to
the throne of Mercia, Kenelm's kingdom
was thrust upon him by the untimely
death of his father in 819 when he was only
eight years old. However, his elder sister
wanted the crown for herself and
persuaded the lad's guardian to murder
him. The treachery was exposed in a
parchment miraculously conveyed to the
pope in Rome by a dove, and Kenelm's
body was recovered and taken to
Winchcombe Abbey for burial. Where his
body was rested each night on
its journey, a healing spring is said to have
sprouted from the ground, and one of these
is passed on the hillside during the walk
from Winchcombe(see Route 18).

Go inside Sapperton's church and
you might find it something of a surprise,
for although of ancient foundation it was
substantially rebuilt in the airy style of
the 18th century by the Atkyns family of
Sapperton Manor. Inside are several
splendid features, including a funerary
tableau depicting Sir Henry Pool with his
wife Anne and their children. So fine is
the work that even the half-turned pages

of their missals appear real. The tiny
St Michael's Church at Duntisbourne
Rouse is also not to be missed, for it has a
beautiful Saxon doorway and striking
herringbone work in its walls. Within are
wall paintings from the 13th century and
misericords that are believed to have been
brought from the abbey at Cirencester.

the ride

1 Emerging from the cul-de-sac lane by
St Kenelm's Church, turn left up the hill,
passing The Bell. The gradient soon eases
as the way approaches a junction, at which
go left again. There follows a pleasant
3 miles (4.8km) along the high ground
above the Frome valley, passing **Parkcorner
Farm**, **Gloucester Lodge**, one of the gates
into the Cirencester Park estate, and, later,
Jackbarrow Farm.

2 There is an opportunity to shorten
the ride at this point, by cutting right
to **Duntisbourne Abbots** and turning right
in the village at a sign to the church.

A steeply curving road through the Cotswold-stone Duntisbourne Abbots

2h45 · **14 MILES** · **22.5 KM** · **LEVEL 1 2 3**

Otherwise, carry on ahead for a further 1.5 miles (2.4km), the road narrower and signed 'Winstone and Cheltenham'. Approaching **Winstone**, the lane bends sharply right into the village. After passing roadside farmhouses, bend left towards **Elkstone** and **Birdslip**, very soon reaching a crossroads beyond the village hall.

3 Now following a sign to Cirencester, keep ahead out of Winstone, where a fold in the open vista on the right conceals the head of the Duntisbourne valley. Before long, the lane turns abruptly right beside the **A417** trunk road, which follows the line of the Roman Ermine Way that ran between Corinium (Cirencester) and Calleva Atrebatum (Silchester). Cycle down to a junction by a bridge.

4 The onward route lies ahead, but to reach **The Five Mile House**, turn left through the underpass and then go right. Come back to this point to continue the ride, climbing in the direction of **Duntisbourne Abbots**. At the end go right, beyond a rise, the lane dropping into the village. However, control the speed of your descent, for there is a tight bend at the bottom of the hill. Climb to a junction and there go left to the church.

5 Follow the lane around **the church**, then turn sharp left to a second junction by a telephone box. The narrow lane to the right leads to a ford that follows the streambed a short distance, a causeway beside it offering a dry-shod crossing. Remounting beyond, carry on to a junction, go right and then left, leaving towards **Middle Duntisbourne** and **Daglingworth**. The way

MAP: OS Explorer 168 Stroud, Tetbury & Malmesbury & 179 Gloucester, Cheltenham & Stroud

START/FINISH: Sapperton: roadside parking beside the church; grid ref SO 947033

TRAILS/TRACKS: country lanes

LANDSCAPE: patterned fields and woodland

PUBLIC TOILETS: none on route

TOURIST INFORMATION: Cirencester, tel 01285 654180

CYCLE HIRE: none locally

THE PUB: The Five Mile House, Duntisbourne Abbots

🛈 Care on narrow lanes; dismount to cross ford

Getting to the start
Perched on the brim of the River Frome's narrow valley, Sapperton lies some 7 miles (11.3km) east of Stroud. The A419 to Cirencester passes just south of the village, and entering via minor lanes, you will find roadside parking at the start of the ride in a cul-de-sac beside the church.

Why do this cycle ride?
It is difficult to go far in the Cotswolds without encountering steep hills, but at Sapperton, the rise and fall of the terrain is relatively gentle, offering for mostly easy cycling along quiet lanes. The route describes a loop through several attractive villages, returning across part of Cirencester Park.

Researched and written by: Dennis Kelsall

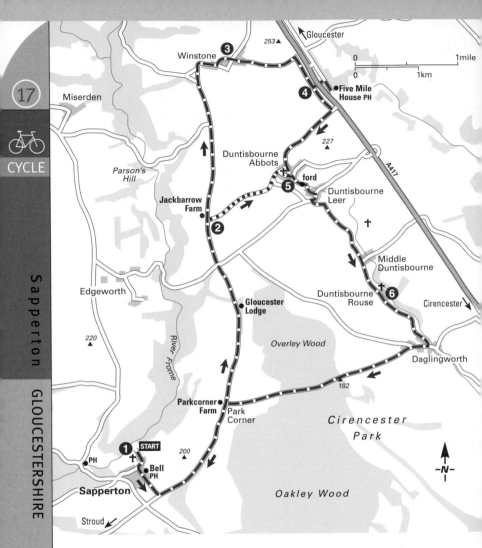

soon becomes wooded and before long reaches Middle Duntisbourne. Keep right on the main lane and, just over the crest of the hill, look for the lych-gate entrance to **Duntisbourne Rouse's** church on the left.

6 Carry on downhill, sticking with the main lane as it twists into Daglingworth. At a junction beside a telephone box, pedal right to **Park Corner** and **Sapperton**. Climb gently away, keeping left when the lane forks at the

edge of the village. There follows an undemanding 0.75 mile (1.2km) climb onto the high ground, entering the **woodland** of the Earl of Bathurst's estate towards the top of the hill. Beyond, the road falls gently to **Park Corner**, where you should go left towards Sapperton. Follow your outward route back to the start, not forgetting that you must turn right to drop back past The Bell.

The Five Mile House

Despite undergoing some modernisation after remaining in a time warp for decades, this 300-year-old country tavern remains a classic, unspoiled gem and well worth lingering in over a pint or two of local Donnington BB. The tiny, bare-boarded bar and the simple tap room up the flagstoned hallway preserve an old-fashioned feel, the latter featuring two ancient high-backed settles, and a wood-burning stove in an old fireplace. Rightly, no food is served in these timeless rooms that are perfect for conversation and quaffing of ale. There is a smart dining room extension to the rear as well as a cellar bar and a family room. Escape to the lovely garden in summer and enjoy the country views.

about the pub

The Five Mile House
Lane's End
Duntisbourne Abbots
Cirencester, Gloucestershire GL7 7JR
Tel: 01285 821432

DIRECTIONS: off A417 north west of Cirencester, signposted Duntisbourne Abbots & Services, turn right, then right again and follow 'no through' road sign

PARKING: 30

OPEN: daily

FOOD: daily

BREWERY/COMPANY: free house

REAL ALE: Donnington BB, Timothy Taylor Landlord, Young's Bitter, guest beer

Food

The freshly prepared food includes lunchtime sandwiches, ham, egg and chips and deep-fried cod and chips. More imaginative evening dishes may feature pork glazed with honey and mustard and neck of lamb with rosemary jelly. Sunday roast lunches.

Family facilities

Well-behaved children are welcome in the family room. Smaller portions of some adult dishes can be prepared.

Alternative refreshment stops

Back in Sapperton, try The Bell at Sapperton (see Route 15, page 79).

☞ Where to go from here

Cirencester is not far away. As well as the Corinium Museum (www.cotswolds.gov.uk) and the largest parish church in England, you can explore Cirencester Park. This fine estate was partly designed by the poet Alexander Pope for Lord Bathurst and can be accessed from Sapperton.

Winchcombe and Sudeley Castle

WALK

A rewarding walk above a thriving Cotswold village and the burial place of Henry's sixth queen, Catherine Parr.

Sudeley Castle

At the end of a long drive just outside Winchcombe is Sudeley Castle. The first castle was built here in 1140 and fragments dating from its earlier, more martial days are still much in evidence. Originally little more than a fortified manor house, by the mid-15th century it had acquired a keep and several courtyards. It became a royal castle after the Wars of the Roses, before being given to Thomas Seymour, Edward VI's Lord High Admiral. Seymour lived at Sudeley with his wife, Catherine Parr – he was her fourth husband. After Seymour was executed for treason the castle passed to Catherine's brother, William, but he was executed too. Queen Mary then gave the property to Sir John Brydges. Sudeley Castle was a Royalist stronghold in the Civil War but was disarmed by the Parliamentarians and left to decay until its purchase by the wealthy Dent brothers in 1863.

Catherine Parr, sixth wife of Henry VIII, is buried in Sudeley's chapel. She was born in 1512, educated in Henry's court and was first married at nine years of age, but widowed six years later. Back at court, she used her influence with the king to protect her second husband, Lord Latimer, from the machinations of courtly politics. When Latimer died in 1543, Catherine, wealthy and well-connected, was an obvious choice of wife for Henry. She looked after him until his death in 1547. She married Seymour and moved to Sudeley, where she died in 1548.

The village of Winchcombe has a considerable history. In Anglo-Saxon times it was a seat of the Mercian kings and the capital of Winchcombshire until the shire's incorporation into Gloucestershire in the 11th century. It became a significant place of pilgrimage due to the abbey established in 798 and dedicated to St Kenelm, the son of its founder, King Kenulf.

The abbey was razed in the Dissolution, but the village's parish church survived and is a fine example of a 'wool church', financed through income from the medieval wool trade. Of particular interest are the amusing gargoyles that decorate its exterior. They are said to be modelled on real local people. Winchcombe also boasts two stimulating small museums: the Folk Museum on the corner of North Street and the Railway Museum on Gloucester Street.

the walk

1 Leave the long stay car park behind the library by a pedestrian access at its far-left corner and turn right along Cowl Lane into the town centre. Turn left onto High Street and then go right in front of **The White Hart** down Castle Street. Soon after crossing a bridge at the bottom, turn left beside **Briar Cottage** along a narrow alley to a field behind. Strike half right across a meadow, still bearing the ridges and furrows of medieval ploughing.

Sudeley Castle is a largely 15th-century reconstruction of the original building

2h00 — 3.75 MILES — 6 KM — LEVEL 123

2 Emerging onto a lane, turn right. At the end of a high stone wall on your right, leave into a field on the left and stride out half right to a gap, about two-thirds the way along the right-hand hedge. Over a **bridge and stile**, bear left to another stile by a gate. Maintain your diagonal course through a break in the middle of the right-hand hedge until you reach a protruding corner and then turn with the fence up the hill to a stile in the overgrown corner.

3 Now climbing more steeply up **Dunn's Hill,** strike a bee-line across the curve of the left-hand fence to a stile beside a gate at the top of the field. Carry on up by the fence and into the next field then bear half right to a stile in the top corner. Keep ahead over more stiles, until the fence on your left turns away.

The Knot Garden at Sudeley Castle

MAP: OS Explorer OL45 The Cotswolds

START/FINISH: Winchcombe: long stay car park on Back Lane; grid ref: SP 023284

PATHS: fields and lanes, 13 stiles

LANDSCAPE: woodland, hills and villages

PUBLIC TOILETS: at car park and on corner of Vine Street

TOURIST INFORMATION: Winchcombe, tel 01242 602925

THE PUB: The White Hart Inn, Winchcombe

Getting to the start

Situated at the junction of the B4632 and B4078, Winchcombe is 6 miles (9.7km) north east of Cheltenham. Park in the long stay car and coach park in Back Lane, which you will find signed from High Street.

Researched and written by:
Dennis Kelsall, Christopher Knowles

4 At that point, swing right down the hill to a stile beside a gate, about half-way along the boundary. A field track leads past a small building protected within a fenced enclosure, marking **St Kenelm's Well**.

5 Passing into the next field, leave the track, bearing right to cross the field to a stile and gate, some two-thirds of the way down the opposite hedge. Keep going downhill, aiming left of **Sudeley Hill Farm** at the bottom to emerge at a road. Turn left and then go right along a lane signed to **Sudeley Lodge** and **Parks Farm**.

6 Opposite a **cottage**, leave right on a footpath falling at the edge of a field. Over a stile, turn right and then left to remain within the field, but leave at the bottom corner. Go forward to a stile on the right and, guided by obvious waymarkers, walk half left, eventually joining a fence to pass **Sudeley Castle** on your right.

7 Passing through two kissing gates into the park, carry on along a contained path to the main drive. Cross to a gate beyond the lawn opposite and bear half right over open grazing, later crossing another track to leave through a kissing gate in the farthest corner. Back in **Castle Street**, turn left and retrace your outward steps past **The White Hart** to the car park.

what to look for

If you go into the church at Winchcombe, note the embroidery behind a screen, said to be the work of Catherine of Aragon, the first wife of Henry VIII. As you descend the hill on the approach to Sudeley Hill Farm, look out for St Kenelm's Well. This is a 19th-century version of a holy well connected with the martyred prince, patron saint of the vanished Winchcombe Abbey.

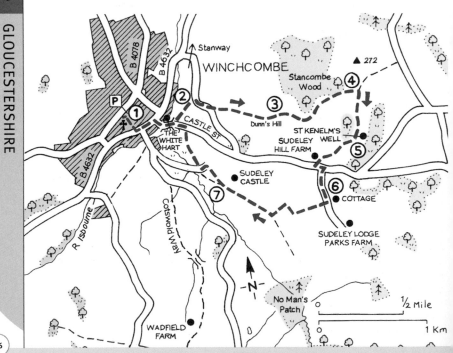

The White Hart Inn

Standing in the heart of this pretty Cotswold town, the black-and-white painted White Hart looks every inch the traditional 16th-century coaching inn it once was. Step inside and the rustic front bar with its wood floor, dark wood pub tables and row of handpumps on the bar maintain the illusion that this is a classic English pub, but throughout the rear dining room and the eight stylishly decorated bedrooms there's a distinct Scandinavian feel. The Swedish owners have brought a cool elegance and minimalist style that permeates the place. The chefs and staff are also from Sweden and Swedish flavours influence the contemporary menu. However, you can still sup local ale, tuck into a rare roast beef baguette, or a home-made pizza in the Stable Bar.

Food

Adventurous diners can enjoy Swedish meatballs, Scandinavian open sandwiches and the speciality smorgasbord platter (cold meats, seafood and salads). Alternatives include crusty baguettes, Gloucestershire pork sausages with mustard mash and onion gravy, and ploughman's platters with home-made chutney. Separate evening restaurant menu. English or Scandinavian breakfast menu served to non-residents.

Family facilities

The pub has a children's licence and they are welcome inside until 9pm. There's a good children's menu and family bedrooms.

Alternative refreshment stops

A large number of possibilities range from pubs to tea rooms and restaurants. If you visit Sudeley Castle, there's a good café.

☛ Where to go from here

Spend some time at Sudeley Castle (www.sudeleycastle.co.uk) or visit the atmospheric ruins of 13th-century Hailes Abbey (www.english-heritage.org.uk). Children will love the Cotswold Farm Park (www.cotswoldfarmpark.co.uk) for the animals, farm safari and pets corner.

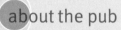

about the pub

The White Hart Inn

High Street, Winchcombe
Gloucestershire GL54 5LJ
Tel: 01242 602359
www.the-white-hart-inn.com

DIRECTIONS: town centre, at the junction of High Street and Castle Street	
PARKING: 12	
OPEN: daily; all day	
FOOD: daily; all day	
BREWERY/COMPANY: Enterprise Inns	
REAL ALE: Goffs White Knight, Wadworth 6X, Greene King IPA & Old Speckled Hen, Bass	
DOGS: welcome in the bar and some bedrooms	
ROOMS: 8 en suite	

CYCLE

Chedworth Roman Villa

Discover a Roman villa
set in a picturesque fold
of the Cotswold Hills.

Roman Villa

Set amid idyllic Cotswold countryside, the
Roman villa at Chedworth is perhaps the
finest discovered in Britain. The area was
well populated during the occupation, and
Corinium (Cirencester) was the second
largest Roman town in the country. The villa
was a chance discovery in 1864 by a
gamekeeper digging to retrieve a lost ferret.
Subsequent excavation has revealed an
extensive site containing wonderfully
preserved features. First built around

120AD, it was enlarged and added to over
the next 300 years, and some 32 rooms
have been identified, including kitchens,
living and dining rooms, latrines and bath
houses as well as outside courtyard and
garden areas. Bathing was an important
element in Roman life, a social occasion
rather than simply a means of keeping
clean. The baths here were obviously well
used, judging by the wear on the floors,
and in addition to cold plunges, there were
wet and dry hot baths. The hypocaust is
clearly revealed, showing how hot air
circulated beneath the floors and within
the walls to provide all-round heating. But
perhaps the most spectacular feature is the
mosaic flooring. The one in the dining room

Chedworth

GLOUCESTERSHIRE

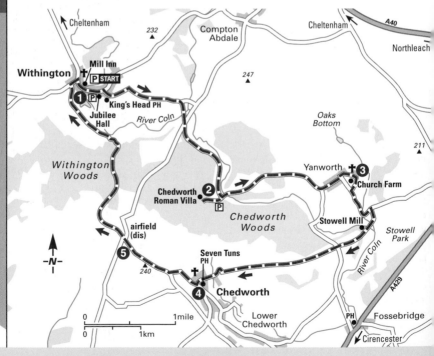

Above: Mosaic at Chedworth Roman Villa
Next page: Foundations of the Roman villa

3h00	10.75 MILES	17.3 KM	LEVEL 123

MAP: OS Explorer OL45 The Cotswolds
START/FINISH: The Mill Inn, Withington (ask permission first); grid ref: SP 032154
TRAILS/TRACKS: country lanes throughout
LANDSCAPE: steeply rolling hills cleaved by deep, wooded valleys
PUBLIC TOILETS: none on route
TOURIST INFORMATION: Cirencester, tel 01285 654180
CYCLE HIRE: none locally
THE PUB: The Mill Inn, Withington
🛈 Several long, steep climbs; care on country lanes

Getting to the start

Some 6 miles (9.7km) south east of Cheltenham, Withington lies in the valley of the River Coln and is most easily reached along a minor lane from the A436. If The Mill Inn is busy, use a car park by the Jubilee Hall on the other side of the old railway bridge.

Why do this cycle ride?

The Coln is one of the prettiest rivers in the Cotswolds and below Withington it winds through a lovely, deep wooded valley. The ride begins in Withington, climbing a shoulder to drop back into the Coln valley, where it passes a Roman villa. The climb to Yanworth is rewarded by medieval wall paintings in its church. On the other side of the valley, the route is via Chedworth before finally returning to Withington past a disused wartime airfield.

Researched and written by: Dennis Kelsall

is particularly brilliant, depicting young boys who represent the four seasons, although sadly, autumn is missing.

the ride

1 From **The Mill Inn** car park, go left between the abutments of a dismantled railway bridge to rise past the entrance to **Jubilee Hall**, which is on the right. At the next turning, go right, signed 'Yanworth' and 'Roman Villa'. After the **King's Head**, leave the village behind, the narrow lane climbing over a hill then falling in a long descent into the Coln valley. There is a fine view ahead across the wolds, although it may be marred for some by the lines of pylons marching over the hills. Cross the river at the bottom and climb to a crossroads. Ahead the lane undulates easily along the wooded edge, shortly reaching a junction where the **Roman villa** is signed off on the right.

2 Rejoin the lane at this point after visiting the villa and re-cross the river, the way signed to Yanworth and Northleach. After another stiff pull, the lane runs more easily over Yanworth Common, eventually reaching a junction. Keep ahead towards **Yanworth**. Pedal through the village, but at the far side where the road bends to Northleach, go left. The lane winds around and down to the church.

3 Carry on down the hill below **Church Farm**, swinging beneath paddocks to a junction. Go left and drop across the bottom of the valley, pulling away steeply beyond to a junction. Turn right towards **Chedworth**, descending back into the vale to re-cross the river by **Stowell Mill**. Another short climb follows, soon levelling to reach a crossroads. Keep ahead, still towards Chedworth, the way rising steadily away. Eventually the lane begins to fall, the

gradient increasing as it twists through sharp bends into Chedworth. Over a stream at the bottom, it is up again, to the **Seven Tuns pub**, opposite which is the church.

4 Continue past the pub and take the lane ahead at the junction above, signed to Withington. At the top of the hill, go right, shortly passing the runways of a **disused airfield**.

5 Carry on at the crossing and then bear right to join a busier road, still following signs to **Withington**. Entering woodland there begins a long descent, which later steepens to a sharp right-hand bend. Emerging from the trees, the way undulates for another 0.75 mile (1.2km) into Withington. Keep with the main lane as it winds through the village, turning right opposite the church to return to The Mill Inn.

The Mill Inn

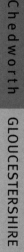
Splendid low-beamed ceilings, large open fireplaces, stone- and oak-panelled walls and worn flagstone floors combine with simple rustic furnishings and country style artefacts to re-create the original atmosphere of this 400-year-old former corn mill and local brewhouse. Right up until 1914 the landlord was listed as an innkeeper and keeper of the watermill. The pub stands in a deep valley on the banks of the River Coln, surrounded by beech and chestnut trees, and it has a lovely riverside garden, complete with ducks, providing an idyllic post-ride setting for peaceful summer drinking. It is one of the few country pubs in the south where you can quaff Samuel Smith's beers.

Food

Menu choices include minty lamb casserole, creamy pork and mushroom pepperpot, steak and ale pie, home-baked crusty baguettes, ploughman's lunches, and a range of 'basket meals' – a food concept said to have originated here in the 1950s.

Family facilities

Families can expect a warm welcome and good provision for children. There's a family area in the pub, youngsters have their own menu and the toilets are equipped with baby-changing facilities. Children should be well supervised in the riverside garden.

Alternative refreshment stops

On the route you will pass the Seven Tuns in Chedworth village and the King's Head at Withington.

☛ Where to go from here

Explore Chedworth Roman Villa, one of the finest Romano-British villas in Britain, or head for Northleach to visit Keith Harding's World of Mechanical Music, a living museum of self-playing musical instruments (www.mechanicalmusic.co.uk).

about the pub

The Mill Inn

Withington, Cheltenham
Gloucestershire GL54 4BE
Tel: 01242 890204

DIRECTIONS: see Getting to the start

PARKING: 60

OPEN: daily

FOOD: daily

BREWERY/COMPANY: Samuel Smith Brewery

REAL ALE: Samuel Smith Best & Old Brewery Bitter

ROOMS: 3 en suite

Chedworth

GLOUCESTERSHIRE

Cotswold Water Park

Abandoned gravel pits create havens for wildlife and opportunities for watersports.

Water Park Wildlife

Overlying the Oxford clay south of Cirencester is a shallow deposit of gravel, which has been exploited since the 1920s for use in building and construction. As individual workings have been abandoned, they have been flooded to create a landscape peppered with almost 100 lakes, causeways and small islands. Left to nature, many of the fringes have developed as marsh and wetland, and the area has become an important site for both resident and migratory water birds. Two of the hides are passed on the cycle ride, and amongst the birds over-wintering here you can expect to see green sandpiper, golden-eye, great northern diver and teal, and if you are lucky, you might even hear the booming of a bittern. In summer you will glimpse many familiar garden birds, also reed and sedge warblers and perhaps a nightingale. Attracted by the water are oystercatchers, shelduck and several species of grebe, and predatory birds such as merlin, harriers and even ospreys make an appearance. Flower-rich meadows attract a variety of butterflies, and dragonflies and damselflies are found around the shores.

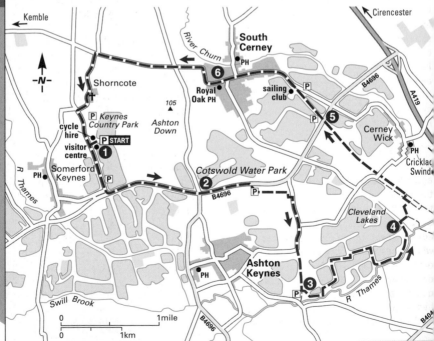

The railway track that takes the ride into South Cerney formed part of the Midland Junction line between Cheltenham and Southampton until its closure during the mid-1960s. Plans are underway to restore part of the line south of Cricklade. Look out for the unusual brick-arched bridges encountered along the way. Their intricate design suggests something more appropriate to the galleries beneath a Roman amphitheatre rather than mere props to carry a road.

the ride

1 Leaving the car park past the visitor centre, follow a shore path to a second smaller car park, there emerging onto **Spratsgate Lane**. Turn left, winding around left again at its end to join Spine Road (West) towards Ashton Keynes. After 1 mile (1.6km) at a crossroads, dismount and cross to continue along Spine Road (East), the busy **B4696** to Cirencester. A few yards/metres along, there is a dedicated cycle track beside it on the left, but be careful for it is bounded by drainage ditches and gutters, with gullies intruding into the pathway.

2 Follow that for another 0.5 mile (800m) to the **Clayhill car park** on the right, again dismounting to reach the entrance. At the back of the car park, a bridlepath leaves to the left, signed to **South Cerney**. Through a gap in the hedge, carry on ahead at the edge of a field, crossing an access road, which leads to a **working gravel pit** (watch out for moving wagons). At the far end, swing onto a track beside the workings. At another quarry road go forward to a break in the hedge opposite, cross a track and continue on the contained path between a lake and

---

2h30 · **10.75 MILES** · **17.3 KM** · **LEVEL 123**

MAP: OS Explorer 169 Cirencester & Swindon

START/FINISH: Keynes Country Park (pay and display car park); grid ref: SU 026958

TRAILS/TRACKS: gravel cycle tracks

LANDSCAPE: low-lying countryside speckled with the lakes of abandoned gravel pits

PUBLIC TOILETS: at car park

TOURIST INFORMATION: Cirencester, tel 01285 654180

CYCLE HIRE: Go By Cycle, Lake 31, Keynes Country Park, Spratsgate Lane, Shorncote, tel: 07970 419208

THE PUB: Royal Oak, South Cerney

🛑 Beware of sleeper barriers and take care on the minor roads and at three main road crossings. Tracks shared with pedestrians and horses and may be muddy after rain

Getting to the start

The Cotswold Water Park lies 4 miles (6.4km) south of Cirencester. From the A419, follow the B4696, continuing ahead at a crossroads north of Ashton Keynes along Spine Road (West). The main car park and visitor centre is then off right along Spratsgate Lane.

Why do this cycle ride?

Cotswold Water Park encompasses some 14,000 acres (5670ha). This route passes both working and abandoned gravel pits (which provide a haven for wildlife). Vast numbers of water birds can be seen. Areas are set aside for water sports and fishing.

Researched and written by: Dennis Kelsall

Fridays Ham Lane, signed 'Waterhay'. It later ends abruptly and you must cross the lane, but be careful, as you are on a blind bend. The ongoing path leads beside a second lake, shortly reaching a junction.

3 The way lies left, marked '**Thames Path**', angularly twisting along old field margins that now separate a succession of lakes. The way passes a bird hide and then through gates demarking the **Manor Brook Lake** fishing area. Over a crossing track the route briefly joins the infant Thames and then passes a small car park. Carry on until you reach the gated pedestrian entrance to **Cleveland Lakes** (where there is another bird hide) and here, go right over a bridge spanning Shire Ditch.

4 Ride on beside a field to meet a broad track and go left towards **South Cerney**. Go left again at the next junction but after 250ys (229m) look for a broad unmarked track on the right. It connects with a parallel **disused railway track**, turn left along it. Tunnelled by trees, the track shortly passes

beneath a viaduct carrying the road from Cerney Wick and continues for another 0.75 mile (1.2km) to reach the B4696 at **Bridge car park**.

5 Cross the road with care. Opposite, the path passes under more arches and resumes its onward course to South Cerney, eventually ending beside the village **sailing club**. The road leads on into the village. Keep ahead at a junction by the old cross towards Ewen and Ashton Keynes, shortly passing the **Royal Oak**, a convenient spot to break the journey.

6 Stay with the road as it meanders past **playing fields** out of the village, before long reaching a crossroads with a busier road. Go forward, signed to Ewen and Kemble, for a little over 0.75 mile (1.2km) then turn off left onto a narrow and, in places, poorly surfaced lane to **Shorncote**. It winds past **Shorncote Manor Farm** and its attendant church, shortly emerging onto Spratsgate Lane. **The Keynes Country Park Visitor Centre** is then less than 0.5 mile (800m) to the left.

House and garden at South Cerney

Royal Oak

Family facilities
Children are welcome in the pub where youngsters have their own menu to choose from. Plenty of space in the safe summer garden.

Alternative refreshment stops
Café at Country Park Visitor Centre; other pubs in South Cerney.

☛ Where to go from here
There's plenty to see and do at Keynes Water Park (www.waterpark.org). Further afield, you can take a ride on the Swindon and Cricklade Railway or visit the Bristol Aero Collection at Kemble (www.bristolaero.i12.com)

In 1997 human remains were found during excavations for an extension to this popular village local close to the Cotswold Water Park. Now thought to have been built on an early Saxon graveyard, the original old cottage first became a pub in 1850. Sympathetic additions over the years have created spacious bars and a dining area, while outside the large and pleasant rear garden features a big terrace and a summer marquee. Come for good-value home-cooked food and rotating real ales from Courage, Adnams, Fuller's and Wychwood breweries.

Food
Traditional pub food includes standard snacks (filled baps, sandwiches and egg and chips), home-made soups, salads, giant Yorkshire puddings with sausages and onion gravy, and lasagne and regular specials such as steak and kidney pie and Barnsley lamb chops.

about the pub

Royal Oak
High Street, South Cerney
Cirencester, Gloucestershire GL7 5UP
Tel: 01285 860298

DIRECTIONS: village signposted off the A419, 3 miles (4.8km) south east of Cirencester; pub located on the left along the road towards Ewen

PARKING: 16

OPEN: daily; all day Friday, Saturday and Sunday

FOOD: daily; all day Friday, Saturday and Sunday

BREWERY/COMPANY: free house

REAL ALE: Courage Best, Marston's Pedigree, guest beers

Around Cutsdean and Ford

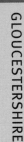
The origins of the Cotswolds, once the focus of England's most valued export, wool.

Lamb's wool to lion's wool

Cutsdean can claim to be the centre of the Cotswolds, according to one theory about the origin of the name 'cotswold'. It may once have been the seat of 'Cod' an Anglo-Saxon chief. His domain would have been his 'dene' and the hilly region in which his domain lay, his 'wolds'. Alternatively, a 'cot' was a sheep fold and 'wolds' were the hills.

Whatever the truth, the sheep remain. The ancestors of the 'Cotswold Lion' probably arrived with the Romans, who valued the sheep's milk and long, dense wool. After the Romans' withdrawal the Saxons continued to farm sheep. The nature of the Cotswolds was perfect: the limestone soil produces a calcium-rich diet;

and the open, wind-blasted wolds suited this heavy-fleeced breed, able to graze all year on abundant herbs and grasses. It is believed that the medieval Cotswold sheep differed a little from its modern counterpart but it was the forelock and the whiteness of its fleece that inspired the nickname, Cotswold Lion, characteristics that persist in the modern sheep.

Demand for the wool was strong in the 18th and 19th centuries and the Cotswold was also prized for its meat and its cross-breeding potential. However, the market for long-stapled wool declined in favour of finer wool, and crop-growing became more attractive to local farmers. By the 1960s, there remained only some 200 animals. The Cotswold Breed Society was reconvened and steps were taken to ensure the sheep's survival. Farmers have since rediscovered the animal's many qualities, and it is no longer quite such a rare sight.

A tree-lined path near Ford

the walk

1 Follow the uphill lane east from the village of Cutsdean for just over a mile (1.6km), to a **crossroads**.

2 Continue along the lane opposite, ignoring after 0.5 mile (800m) the turning off left to **Scarborough Farm**. Later rising beyond a dip, the track eventually emerges from woodland into open ground.

3 Keep ahead past a waymark to a lateral boundary a little further on and go through the right-hand one of the two openings before you. Continue at the field edge with a wall on your left for some 500yds (457m) to a **waypost** and bear right across the field towards a **plantation**.

4 Pass through the trees, then as you emerge on the far side, double back sharp right on a track beside them. Carry on for a mile (1.6km) to **Ford Hill Farm**, leaving past the farmhouse along its drive to meet a road.

5 Opposite, the imposing gateway to **Jackdaw Castle** heralds a long metalled drive beside 'The Gallops'.

6 Shortly after dropping past the stables, half hidden behind a banking over to the right, look for a waymark and sign directing you right across the **training track**. If the horses are running, heed well the warning notice. Continue downhill on the

| 2h45 | 5.75 MILES | 9.3 KM | LEVEL 123 |

MAP: OS Explorer OL45 The Cotswolds

START/FINISH: Cutsdean village or beside lane to the east; grid ref: SP 087302 (Cutsdean village centre)

PATHS: tracks, fields and lane, 5 stiles

LANDSCAPE: open wold, farmland, village

PUBLIC TOILETS: none on route

TOURIST INFORMATION: Stow-on-the-Wold, tel 01451 831082

THE PUB: The Plough Inn, Ford

Getting to the start

Cutsdean is 4 miles (6.4km) west of Winchcombe. The nearest classified road, the B4077, passes through Ford, just to the south. Parking in the hamlet is very limited, but a wide verge beside the lane to the east along which the walk begins offers other possibilities. Ensure you do not impede traffic flow or block field accesses.

Researched and written by:
Dennis Kelsall, Christopher Knowles

St James Church at Cutsdean

far drive, emerging at its end onto a road in front of **The Plough Inn** at Ford.

7 Walk down the hill, turning off right just before the river at the entrance of a drive. Over a stile before you, follow the top of a wooded bank beside **paddocks** behind the house, the path later curving left amongst the trees to a stile.

8 Turn half right along the field, crossing the head of a muddy stream to gain the left corner. Over a stile, follow the field edge left, eventually passing the **church** to emerge in **Cutsdean**. The lane along which the walk began lies to the right.

what to look for

Horses are very important to the local economy. The countryside is covered in 'gallops', earthy tracks where racehorses are exercised in safety. You'll also notice a large number of jumps, like the hurdles at a proper racecourse. Many racehorses are bred here, and some may get to race at nearby Cheltenham, home to the pre-eminent steeple-chase course in the country and host to the huge Cheltenham Festival racing event.

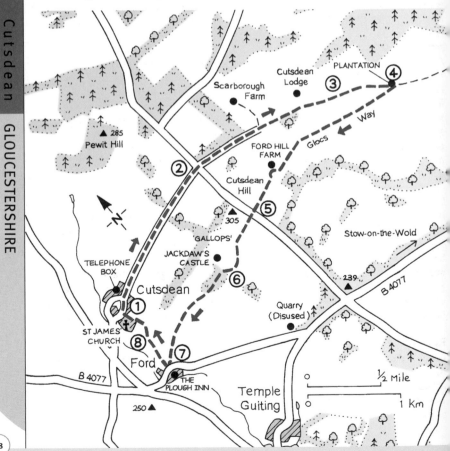

The Plough Inn

Long a favourite of Cotswold ramblers, racing enthusiasts and lovers of the traditional English pub, the interior of the idyllic little Plough Inn, with its warming open fires, sturdy pine furnishings and lively conversation, has all the atmosphere you could wish for. With its origins dating back to the 13th century, the simply furnished bars recall the pub's past days as a farmhouse with flagstone floors, heavy beams and a huge inglenook. There's a comprehensive menu that features fresh local produce and excellent Donnington ales are on tap. Plus there's a walled garden for fine-weather eating and drinking. The pub is famous for its traditional asparagus feasts every May to June, when the first asparagus spears to be sold at auction in the Vale of Evesham usually end up on plates at The Plough. There are three comfortable en suite bedrooms.

about the pub

The Plough Inn
Ford, Cheltenham
Gloucestershire GL54 5RU
Tel: 01386 584215
www.theploughinnatford.co.uk

DIRECTIONS: beside the B4077, 5 miles (8km) west of Stow-on-the-Wold
PARKING: 50
OPEN: daily; all day
FOOD: daily; all day Saturday & Sunday
BREWERY/COMPANY: Donnington Brewery
REAL ALE: Donnington BB & SBA
DOGS: allowed in the bar
ROOMS: 3 en suite

Cutsdean

GLOUCESTERSHIRE

Food

Blackboards list the day's menu, the interesting choice may include home-made soups and patés, steak and Guinness pie, home-baked gammon and eggs, beef and mushrooms in red wine, pork tenderloin in mustard sauce and fresh Donnington trout. Good lunchtime snacks include baguettes and sandwiches.

Family facilities

Children of all ages are welcome in the pub. High chairs, small cutlery and smaller portions of main menu dishes are all available. The safe rear garden has a play fort.

Alternative refreshment stops

Nearby Winchcombe has plenty of pubs and tea rooms.

☛ Where to go from here

Explore the atmospheric ruins of Hailes Abbey, a great medieval pilgrimage abbey built in the 13th century. Take a trip to Sudeley Castle, once home to Queen Catherine Parr, with its magnificent award-winning gardens and exhibitions (www.sudeleycastle.co.uk). Children will enjoy the Cotswold Farm Park at Guiting Power.

A circuit from Guiting Power

A gentle ramble from a typical village with an atypical place name and atypical ownership.

What's in a name?

It is remarkable how much detailed history is available about English villages, even ones, like Guiting Power, that are distinguished only by their comeliness. Looking from the village green, surrounded by stone cottages, with its church and secluded manor house, it is easy to imagine that very little has changed here in 1,000 years. The eccentric name comes from the Saxon word 'gyte-ing', or torrent, and indeed the name was given not only to Guiting Power but also to neighbouring Temple Guiting, which in the 12th century was owned by the Knights Templars. Guiting Power though, was named after the 13th-century pre-eminent family the Le Poers.

Farmland was only enclosed in 1798, allowing small landowners such as a local tailor called John Williams, who owned 12 acres (4.86ha) in the form of medieval strips scattered thoughout the parish, to finally consolidate their possessions.

By the end of the 19th century the rural depression had reduced the population to 431, and it continued to decline throughout the 20th century. Nonetheless, it is recorded that apart from public houses (at least four), there were two grocers, two bakers, two tailors, two carpenters, two policemen and a blacksmith.

There are still two pubs in Guiting Power but everything else, apart from the post office and a single grocery store, has disappeared. The village is unusual in that it hasn't succumbed to the inflationary effects of second homeowners from the cities pushing local housing beyond the reach of existing locals. Much of this is down to the far-sightedness of Moya Davidson, a resident in the 1930s, who purchased cottages to be rented out locally. It has meant that younger people are able to stay in the village to live and work and there are still a few families here who can trace their roots back in Guiting Power for several generations.

what to look for

The Norman doorway in Guiting church is an exceptionally rich golden hue. In Naunton, if you stroll back from the Black Horse Inn towards the church on the opposite side of the river then you will be rewarded with a view of a large but charming 17th-century dovecote. Many villages had dovecotes for eggs and winter meat.

A dovecote in Naunton dating from c1600

2h30 | **5.25 MILES** | **8.4 KM** | **LEVEL 123**

the walk

1 From the **village hall** car park, walk down the road to the green. Cross to a lane opposite that quickly disintegrates to a track. At the bottom, go through a kissing gate on the right and walk away, following a stream down to a bridge. Climb the opposite bank to another kissing gate. However, ignore that in favour of a stile on the right.

2 Swing left beside the hedge, keeping ahead where it later turns away to reach another stile. Go forward, crossing more stiles to pass **Little Windrush Farm**, and walk out to a lane. Follow it right to a junction and go right again down to a **bridge**. Then, when the lane turns sharply right, leave along a track on the left.

Looking down to the village of Naunton in the Windrush Valley

MAP: OS Explorer OL45 The Cotswolds

START/FINISH: Guiting Power: car park outside village hall (small fee); grid ref: SP 094246

PATHS: fields, tracks and country lanes, 10 stiles

LANDSCAPE: woodland, hills and village

PUBLIC TOILETS: none on route

TOURIST INFORMATION: Stow-on-the-Wold, tel 01451 831082

THE PUB: The Hollow Bottom, Guiting Power

Getting to the start

Guiting Power can be found a short way north of the B4068, 6 miles (9.7km) west of Stow-in-the-Wold. A car park in front of the village hall near the church is signed from the main lane passing through the village.

Researched and written by:
Dennis Kelsall, Christopher Knowles

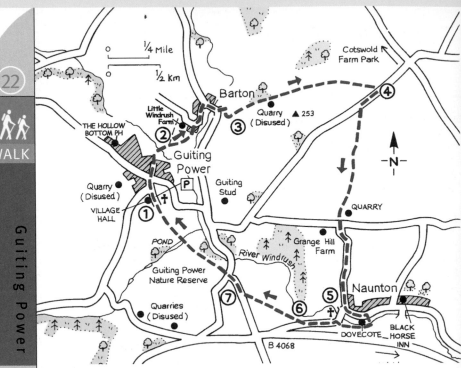

3 Branch right at a fork and continue climbing to a gate. As the track splits again, keep left and follow it for about a mile (1.6km) to a road.

4 Turn right, but after 250yds (229m), take another track leaving on the left. Emerging at a junction by **Grange Hill Farm**, cross to the lane opposite and follow it downhill for a mile (1.6km) into **Naunton**.

5 Go left in the village, passing a **Baptist chapel** and shortly reaching a telephone box . A narrow lane on the right winds down past **Naunton's historic dovecote**. Keep right at the bottom, cross a stream and go through a gate. Turn right once more and follow the stream to the main lane by the **parish church**, which climbs left out of Naunton.

6 After 0.25 mile (400m) mount a stile on the right and turn left, maintaining your height around the top edge of a field to another stile. Walk ahead into the next field and keep the same line across, aiming for a **copse** of trees in the middle distance. At the far side, go forward with the trees on your left, leaving through a gate beyond them onto a lane.

7 Turn right down to a junction and cross to the field opposite. Strike out, staying roughly parallel with the hedge to the right. Over a stile in the middle of the far boundary, go down a stepped bank to find a **bridge** spanning a small stream emanating from a pond. Climb to the field above and keep the same direction to the far side, where a final field separates you from the church and the car park, just beyond.

The Hollow Bottom

Owned by a syndicate that includes former jockey Peter Scudamore, this rustic, 18th-century Cotswold-stone pub has a distinct horse-racing theme, and is frequented by the racing fraternity associated with Cheltenham. The place really buzzes with activity if a local stable has a big winner! In the simple public bar you can watch the racing on the TV while supping a pint of Hooky by the log fire and tucking into some good, traditional pub food. Nooks and crannies in the welcoming lounge bar lend themselves to an intimate drink or meal, and there's a separate dining room. The place to head for on fine summer days is the pleasant rear garden where tables look out across rolling fields. Cosy bedrooms make this village local a good base from which to explore the Cotswolds.

about the pub

The Hollow Bottom
Guiting Power, Cheltenham
Gloucestershire GL54 5UX
Tel: 01451 850392
www.hollowbottom.com

DIRECTIONS: at the north western end of the village, go down to the village green and follow the lane left

PARKING: 8

OPEN: daily; all day

FOOD: daily; snacks all day

BREWERY/COMPANY: free house

REAL ALE: Hook Norton Bitter, Fuller's London Pride, guest beer

DOGS: welcome inside the pub

ROOMS: 4 bedrooms (3 en suite)

Guiting Power

GLOUCESTERSHIRE

Family facilities
Children have their own menu, smaller portions are available and there are high chairs, baby-changing facilities, small cutlery and activities provided.

Alternative refreshment stops
Guiting Power's other pub is the Farmers Arms, just off the village green. Naunton has the very pleasant Black Horse Inn.

Food
Traditional meals take in filled baguettes, sausage and mash, ploughman's lunches and home-cooked ham, egg and chips. Freshly made daily specials may include grilled marlin, poached monkfish, bison steak in brandy sauce, and calves' liver with bacon and mash.

☞ Where to go from here
The Cotswold Farm Park at Guiting Power (www.cotswoldfarmpark.co.uk) has nearly 50 breeding herds and flocks of the rarest British breeds of cattle, sheep, pigs, goats and waterfowl – see a Bagot goat, cuddle a lamb or stroke a mighty Longhorn ox.

The Upper Windrush Valley and the Slaughters

Explore the countryside around two of the Cotswolds most famous villages.

The Slaughters

Bubbling from a spring in a secluded fold of the Cotswold hills, the River Eye embarks on a short but pretty journey past the Slaughters before becoming lost in the River Windrush, just a couple of miles further on below Bourton-on-the-Water. But for their unashamed loveliness, the two tiny villages would probably have escaped the notice of the modern world. Despite their popularity, they have remained

unspoiled, resisting large car parks and commercial gift shops. At Lower Slaughter, you can visit a corn mill, which, although dating only from the 19th century, continues the tradition of a succession of earlier mills that have occupied the site since the Normans arrived on these shores. It houses a small shop, tea room, and museum which shows how grist milling has been carried out over the centuries.

Despite the proximity of the two villages, Upper Slaughter displays a completely different character to its neighbour. The cottages around The Square were reconstructed in 1906 by the great architect Sir Edward Lutyens, the designer

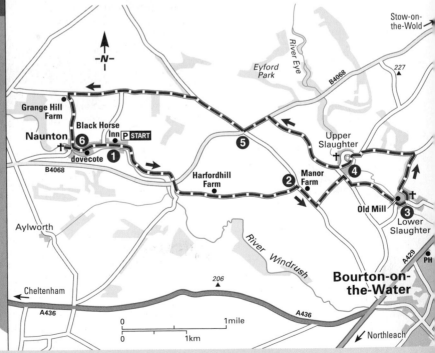

The River Eye passing through Upper Slaughter

of New Delhi, while a little earlier, the Victorian vicar of the Norman church, the Reverend Francis E Witts wrote *The Diary of a Cotswold Parson*.

Back in Naunton, the impressive dovecote is a rare survivor of its type, the roof sporting four gables and topped by a louvre to permit access by the birds. It is thought to date from around 1600 and was built to provide the lord of the manor with fresh meat during the winter months.

the ride

1 Starting with the pub on your left, follow the lane out of the village, as yet pedalling easily along the bottom of the **Windrush valley**. At a crossroads with the B4068, the honeymoon comes to an end as you take the leftmost of the two lanes opposite. Tunnelled in trees it climbs steeply away, but before long you can start changing up through the gears as the gradient levels past **Harfordhill Farm**. Your exertion is rewarded by a fine view across the wolds as you continue to a junction.

2 Go right past **Manor Farm**, and then left at the next turning, signed to Upper and Lower Slaughter. Free-wheeling down, watch your speed, for there is a T-junction at the bottom where you should go right to **Lower Slaughter**. Keep with the main lane as it shortly bends left in front of a junction and sweeps around beside the River Eye into the centre of the village.

CYCLE

The Slaughters

GLOUCESTERSHIRE

3h00 | **9 MILES** | **14.5 KM** | **LEVEL 1 2 3**

MAP: OS Explorer OL 45 The Cotswolds
START/FINISH: The Black Horse Inn, Naunton (ask permission first); grid ref: SP 234119
TRAILS/TRACKS: country lanes
LANDSCAPE: rolling Cotswold countryside between the valleys of the Windrush and Eye
PUBLIC TOILETS: none on route
TOURIST INFORMATION: Stow-on-the-Wold, tel 01451 831082
CYCLE HIRE: none locally
THE PUB: The Black Horse Inn, Naunton
🛈 Several stiff and one steep ascent, and a long downhill stretch. Suitable for fitter, older family groups.

Getting to the start

Naunton is located just off the B4068, 4.5 miles (7.2km) west of Stow-on-the-Wold. Leaving the main road, follow a narrow lane through the village to find The Black Horse Inn, from which the ride begins.

Why do this cycle ride?

The twin villages of the Slaughters are the epitome of the Cotswold village, and although both can become unbearably crowded on a fine weekend during the summer, they display nothing but charm on a quieter day. Inevitably, the ride encounters a succession of hills, but take your time, and you will discover scenic beauty in this pastoral countryside that is often missed when travelling by car.

Researched and written by: Dennis Kelsall

3 At a junction in front of **St Mary's Church**, go left, passing through the more recent part of the village and the cricket green before climbing steadily away.

5 Turn right on a lane, signed to **Cotswold Farm Park**, enjoying a much easier 0.5 mile (800m). At a fork, bear left to Guiting Power and Winchcombe, the gently

After 0.33 mile (500m) at a bend, turn sharp left to **Upper Slaughter**, pedalling over a gentle rise before dropping to a junction. To the left the lane falls more steeply, winding sharply to a bridge at the bottom of the hill. Climb away on the far side to a small raised green at the heart of the village, above which to the right stands the **church**. Don't leave without having a look at the **ford**, which lies over the hill behind the church. The high ground opposite was the site of an early Norman stronghold.

4 The route continues with the main lane through the village to a junction. Go right towards Cheltenham. There follows a prolonged pull out of the valley, which eventually eases to a junction with the **B4068**. To the left the climb resumes for another 0.25 mile (400m) to a crossroads.

undulating road offering more expansive views to the south. Go past the first turning off left, signed to Naunton, continuing for a further 0.5 mile (800m) to a second turning, also on the left by **Grange Hill Farm**. An unmarked narrow lane, it drops steeply into the valley. Go carefully as it winds sharply to a junction at the edge of Naunton.

6 The way back to The Black Horse Inn is to the left, but first have a look at the **church**, which lies a short distance along to the right. As you return to the pub, another deviation is merited, this time, turning right just after the **Baptist church** to see Naunton's historic **dovecote**.

A cyclist passes through Lower Slaughter village without encountering other traffic

The Black Horse Inn

The setting is a typical Cotswold village sunk deep in the beautiful Windrush Valley, much beloved of ramblers, cyclists and locals alike. Original flagstones, blackened beams, open log fires, simple tables and chairs and fine oak pews exude rural charm in the main bar while the lounge offers a smaller, snugger retreat. Built of honey-coloured stone and dating from the 1870s, the pub is renowned for its home-cooked food, Donnington real ales and utterly peaceful bed and breakfast.

Food

Dishes range from ploughman's, filled baguettes and jacket potatoes to some accomplished main dishes: steak and kidney pudding, grilled trout, chicken breast with Stilton and bacon, salmon fillet in saffron sauce, and local game in season. There's also the day's selection of 'sinful sweets'!

Family facilities

Families are welcome inside the pub. There's a children's menu, smaller portions of adult meals and high chairs are available.

Alternative refreshment stops

Hotels for lunches and cream teas in both the Slaughters; café at The Mill in Lower Slaughter.

☛ Where to go from here

Spend some time in Bourton-on-the-Water. Children will enjoy the fabulous toy collection and the cars at the Cotswold Motoring Museum and Toy Collection (www.cotswold-motor-museum.com), the perfect replica of a Cotswold village at the Model Village, and a visit to Birdland Park and Gardens, a natural setting of woodland, river and gardens inhabited by more than 500 birds.

about the pub

The Black Horse Inn
Naunton, Stow-on-the-Wold
Gloucestershire GL54 3AD
Tel: 01451 850565
www.blackhorsenaunton.com

DIRECTIONS: see Getting to the Start

PARKING: 12

OPEN: daily; all day Saturday & Sunday

FOOD: no food Monday evening

BREWERY/COMPANY: Donnington Brewery

REAL ALE: Donnington BB & SBA

ROOMS: 1 en suite

A loop walk from Northleach

WALK

A modest Cotswold village is home to an unusual museum.

Mechanical music museum

Northleach is a small country village with a fascinating and rather unusual museum, Keith Harding's World of Mechanical Music, which is one of those eccentricities that has, by happenstance, ended up here in Northleach.

The World of Mechanical Music is in the High Street at Oak House, a former wool house, pub and school. There are daily demonstrations of all manner of mechanical musical instruments, as well as musical boxes, clocks and automata. Some of the instruments, early examples of 'canned' music, date back more than 200 years. The presentation is simultaneously erudite and light-hearted. (You may also listen to early, live recordings of concerts given by some of the great composers including Gershwin and Grieg.) This is something more than a museum – both serious historical research and highly accomplished repairs are carried out here.

Northleach itself, like Cirencester and Chipping Campden, was one of the key medieval wool-trading centres of the Cotswolds and therefore also one of the most important towns in Europe. Though once on a crossroads of the A40 and the Fosse Way, neither now passes through the town. The completion of the A40 bypass in the mid-1980s left the town centre a quiet and very attractive place to visit. The main street is lined with houses, some half-timbered, dating from between the 16th and 19th centuries. Many of these retain their ancient 'burgage' plots at the rear that would originally have served as market gardens. Above the market square

is a tiny maze of narrow lanes, overlooked by the Church of St Peter and St Paul, the town's impressive 15th-century Perpendicular 'wool church'. Its features include an array of brasses commemorating the wool merchants on whose wealth the church and town were founded.

the walk

1 From Northleach square, with the **church** behind you, turn left and walk along the main street past **The Wheatsheaf Inn** to traffic lights on the A429 by the former **Correction House**. Cross with care to the lane opposite, but then immediately after passing the austere old Police Station, turn through a gate on the right into a field.

2 Strike a diagonal line to the far corner, maintaining the same course across subsequent fields as you climb towards **Hampnett church**. Emerging onto a lane at the top, go left.

3 The route leaves the lane almost immediately along a concrete track that drops to the left. At a junction beyond a group of **farm buildings**, go left again, climbing towards a gate. Keep on to reach a road, crossing it to continue along the track facing you. It leads to a second road.

Right: Displays in Keith Harding's World of Mechanical Music in Northleach

Left: The 15th-century church of St Peter and St Paul in Northleach has a range of brasses commemorating the town's wool merchants

1h45 · **4 MILES** · **6.4 KM** · **LEVEL 123**

MAP: OS Explorer OL45 The Cotswolds
START/FINISH: Northleach village square; grid ref: SP 113145
PATHS: fields, tracks and pavement, muddy after rain, 3 stiles
LANDSCAPE: valley track, wolds and villages
PUBLIC TOILETS: in village square
TOURIST INFORMATION: Cirencester, tel 01285 654180
THE PUB: The Wheatsheaf Inn, Northleach

Getting to the start

Northleach lies beside the Fosse Way, the A429, near its junction with the A40; 10 miles (16.1km) north east of Cirencester and 12 miles (19.3km) south east of Cheltenham. If the central car park in the square is full, you should have little difficulty in finding suitable roadside parking.

Researched and written by:
Dennis Kelsall, Christopher Knowles

4 Now turn left and walk over a crossroads to meet the busy A429. Cross with great care to a path opposite, which shortly takes you past **Winterwell Barn**. It then continues as a track to end at yet another road.

5 Cross to a field track, not the adjacent drive to Cats Abbey Farm, and follow this for a little over 0.33 mile (500m) to find a gap in the left hedge. Follow the left field margin down, **Northleach** soon coming into view. Cross a stile at the bottom corner and continue downhill leaving through a gate at the bottom, beside a playground.

what to look for

Leaving Northleach, look out for some interesting old houses. Walton House, for example, was formerly the King's Head, an important inn on the old London to Gloucester route. Further on, set back from the road, are the buildings of the old brewery.

6 Wind between it and a **tennis court**, leaving across a stream behind the court. Follow a passage up between houses, turning left at the top to return to the starting point.

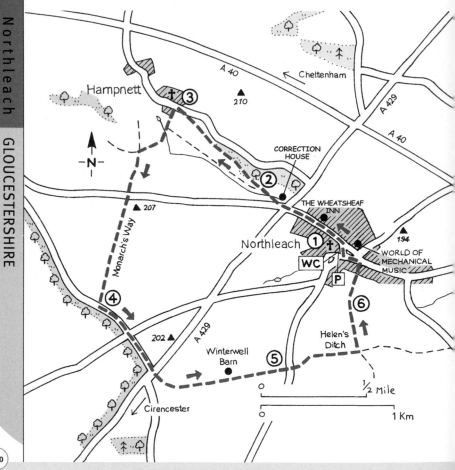

The Wheatsheaf Inn

Looking out across the main street to the famous parish church in this celebrated wool town, the mellow stone Wheatsheaf, built as a coaching inn during the 17th century, is a comfortable and civilised place to retreat to after this Cotswold ramble. In the friendly bar you'll find flagstones on the floor, a blazing log fire in the grate, lots of old wood and beams, and top-notch Hooky beer on handpump. The adjoining dining room is a little more formal, with large, neatly laid-up tables, prints and mirrors on the walls and a classy feel. There are excellent wines, smartly refurbished en suite bedrooms, and a fine terraced garden full of flowers for summer alfresco lunching.

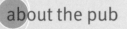

about the pub

The Wheatsheaf Inn
West End, Northleach
Cheltenham, Gloucestershire
GL54 3EZ
Tel: 01451 860244
www.wheatsheafatnorthleach.com

DIRECTIONS: on the main village street

PARKING: 15

OPEN: daily; all day March-October

FOOD: daily

BREWERY/COMPANY: free house

REAL ALE: Wadworth 6X, Hook Norton Bitter, guest beer

DOGS: welcome inside

ROOMS: 8 en suite

Food
The short lunch menu lists home-made soup, smoked trout and horseradish sandwich (with chips and salad), beer-battered haddock and smoked chicken Caesar salad. There is a more elaborate evening menu and good blackboard specials, perhaps local sausages with mustard mash, and turbot fillet with watercress salad.

Family facilities
Children of all ages are welcome at the Wheatsheaf. Smaller portions of the main menu dishes are available and there are high chairs for younger family members.

Alternative refreshment stops
Although only fairly small Northleach has two other pubs, the Red Lion and the Sherborne Arms.

☛ Where to go from here
Visit Chedworth Roman Villa to view the remains of one of the finest Romano-British villas in Britain, replete with fine 4th-century mosaics, two bath houses and a temple with spring.

A circuit from Bibury

The outer charm of a weavers' village conceals miserable former working conditions.

Weaving industry

Arlington Row is the picturesque terrace of cottages that led William Morris to refer to Bibury as the most beautiful village in England. It was originally built, it is thought, in the late 14th century, to house sheep belonging to Osney Abbey in Oxford. Following the Dissolution the land was sold off and the sheep houses converted to weavers' cottages. Before mechanisation transformed the wool weaving industry, most weaving took place in the houses of the poor. Firstly, women and children spun the wool either at home or at the workhouse. Then it was transferred to the houses of the weavers, who worked on handlooms at home at low rates.

Strictly speaking, much of what is considered picturesque in Bibury is in the neighbouring village of Arlington, but they are now indistinguishable. Apart from Arlington Row, there is plenty to enjoy in the village, especially the church, which has Saxon origins and is set in pretty gardens. Across the bridge is the old mill, open to the public. Nearby Ablington has an enchanting group of cottages, threaded by the River Coln. A minor classic, *A Cotswold Village* (1898), which describes local life in the late 19th century, was written by J Arthur Gibbs, the squire who lived at Ablington Manor. You pass the walls of the manor on the walk. Close by, further into the village, are a couple of beautiful 18th-century barns.

the walk

1 From the parking area opposite **Arlington Mill**, walk along the main road in the direction of Cirencester. Some 50yds (46m) after **The Catherine Wheel**, and opposite a telephone box, turn right along a narrow lane towards **Arlington Farm**. Through gates, keep left at a fork, pass the farmhouse and walk on at the edge of a field. Over a drive, maintain the same line across successive fields, eventually passing a house to emerge onto a lane.

2 Turn right and walk down to a junction, there going right into **Ablington**. Some 30yds (27m) after crossing a bridge, double back sharp left onto a minor lane, following a mill leat past cottages. Degenerating to a track beyond a gate, it meanders pleasantly for 0.5 mile (800m) before reaching a second gate.

3 Entering a field, curve right to follow a sinuous route along the base of a valley, passing through occasional gates and eventually going by **Downs Barn**.

Arlington Row in Bibury was where weavers once lived and worked

2h45 — 6.25 MILES — 10.1 KM — LEVEL 1 2 3

MAP: OS Explorer OL45 The Cotswolds

START/FINISH: Bibury: opposite Arlington Mill; grid ref: SP 114068

PATHS: field tracks and a lane, may be muddy in places, 6 stiles

LANDSCAPE: exposed wolds, valley, villages and streams

PUBLIC TOILETS: opposite river on main street, close to Arlington Row

TOURIST INFORMATION: Cirencester, tel 01285 654180

THE PUB: The Catherine Wheel, Bibury

Getting to the start

Bibury is on the B4425, almost midway between Cirencester – 7 miles (11.3km) and Burford – 10 miles (16.1km). There is a roadside car park in the centre of the village by the bridge opposite Arlington Mill on the southern bank of the river.

Researched and written by:
Dennis Kelsall, Christopher Knowles

WALK

Bibury

GLOUCESTERSHIRE

4 A track now develops, bearing right and ascending towards the head of a side valley. When the main track subsequently veers right, keep ahead on a lesser track that winds left to a **gate**. Follow it out to a lane.

5 Turn right, but after 300yds (274m) at a right-hand bend, leave onto a track ahead, the **Salt Way**, and follow it for 0.5 mile (800m) to **Saltway Barn**.

6 Through a gate just before the scatter of buildings, keep left where the track splits. Walk past sheds on the left and go through an opening into the corner of a field. A track to the right continues at the edge of successive fields for almost 0.75 mile (1.2km) before meeting a junction.

7 Turn right through a gate, remaining with the new track past **Hale Barn** and then a junction off to **Bibury Farm**. Carry on towards Bibury whose buildings soon come into view ahead. Beyond a house, the way becomes partly metalled and eventually winds down to the main road at the edge of the village. Turn right and then left as if to walk down to Bibury Court, but instead, immediately leave through a gap in the low right-hand wall by a

telephone box. Follow the street ahead past cottages, turning right at the bottom in front of the church to return to the main road. Go left, but then cross the river at the first bridge to **Arlington Row**. At the end of the terrace of cottages, swing right on a path that follows a stream back to Arlington Mill.

what to look for

Ablington Manor is to your right (behind high stone walls) as you cross the bridge in the village. Look out, too, not just for the 18th-century barns (mentioned above) but also for Ablington House, guarded by a pair of lions that once stood at the Houses of Parliament.

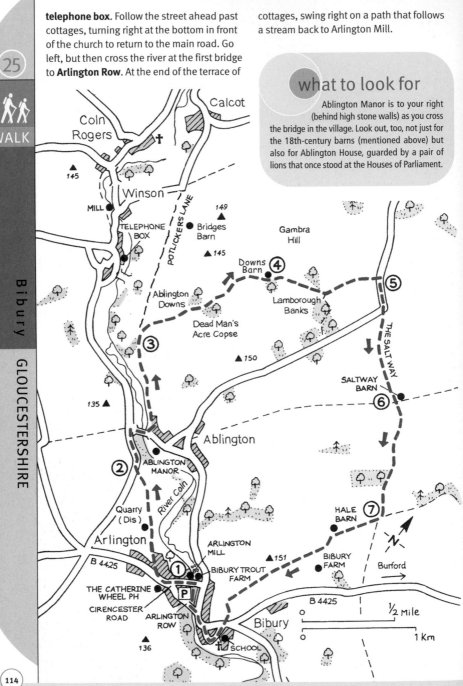

The Catherine Wheel

Fruit trees grow against the wall at each side of the entrance to this 500-year-old stone pub situated in this classic Cotswold village, a short stroll from Arlington Row (NT) – a group of ancient cottages – and the River Coln. Inside, the three small, low-beamed rooms have the mellow atmosphere of an unpretentious, unspoiled local. Most of the drinking is done in the first bar, which has a log fire in winter and ceiling beams taken from old wooden ships, when they were broken up in Gloucester dock – an example of 15th-century recycling. Most of the eating takes place in the other two rooms, both with wood-burning stoves, pictures of old Bibury, and traditional pub furnishings. Summer attractions include colourful hanging baskets and neatly tended terraced lawns full of picnic benches. There are four en suite bedrooms in well converted outhouses.

Food

Traditional home-made pub food ranges from lunchtime snacks such as filled jacket potatoes, hot and cold baguettes and plaice and chips to Thai fishcakes, lambs' liver and bacon, paella and Bibury trout.

Family facilities

Children are welcome away from the bar. You will find a children's menu, high chairs, baby-changing facilities, and activities to keep children amused. Lovely rear garden with rabbits constantly in residence.

Alternative refreshment stops

The Swan Hotel has a good restaurant and also serves teas. A variety of snacks are available at Bibury Trout Farm and at the mill.

about the pub

The Catherine Wheel

Bibury, Cirencester
Gloucestershire GL7 5ND
Tel: 01285 740250

DIRECTIONS: just up from the car park towards Cirencester	
PARKING: 25	
OPEN: daily; all day	
FOOD: daily	
BREWERY/COMPANY: Eldridge Pope	
REAL ALE: Adnams Bitter, Wadworth 6X	
DOGS: allowed in the garden only	
ROOMS: 4 en suite	

☛ Where to go from here

Bibury Trout Farm is a working farm where children can feed the fish and even catch their own – all tackle provided. There are also plenty of activities at the Cotswold Water Park and Keynes Country Park to keep children amused (www.waterpark.org).

The Leach and Coln valleys

Wander the wolds between rivers that feed the upper reaches of the River Thames.

Ancient trackways

Salt was once a highly valued commodity, attracting taxes and being paid as wages. Important not only as a condiment, it was demanded in large quantities during the Middle Ages to preserve meat and fish for use during the winter. Produced at certain spots along the coast, where seawater could be panned and concentrated into brine, salt was also found naturally as geological deposits, such places often incorporating 'wich' within their name. The salt was traded across the country, carried by packhorse along routes which became known as 'Salt Ways'.

It is often assumed that Britain had no roads before the Romans arrived, but this is far from the truth and there is abundant evidence of a complex pattern of prehistoric paths and trackways. But the stability of the Roman Empire depended upon efficient communications, and it was they who first laid out a formal network of paved roads throughout the country. The pattern radiated from Londinium, linking the major military bases, but other routes quickly followed connecting the various towns and settlements as local trade developed. Akeman Street ran for more than 75 miles (121km) between Verulamium (St Albans) and Corinium (Cirencester), and at least in part followed a pre-existing British trackway. As with many Roman roads, it continued in use after the occupation and large sections are incorporated into today's road system.

the ride

1 The crossroads in the middle of Coln St Aldwyns is marked by a sturdy spreading chestnut tree. Begin the ride along the lane signed to Quenington and Fairford, passing the **New Inn**. Leaving the village, cycle over the River Coln and climb to a crossroads at the edge of **Quenington**. Go left onto **Fowlers Hill** and drop back into the valley, following signs to Southrop and Lechlade as you bend past a junction to re-cross the Coln. After a bit of a pull, the lane gently rises over open down, following the line of an ancient **salt way**. Pedal on for some 2.5 miles (4km), following signs for Southrop past junctions, before eventually losing height to a 'Give Way' junction.

2 Go left, gaining height along a gentle fold in the rolling hillside. Stay with the main lane as it later turns to rise over the hill, winding down on the other side into **Southrop**. Carry on past the village hall and **The Swan**, the street slotted between high-kerbed pavements and now signed to Filkins.

3 After dropping away and crossing the second river of the journey, the Leach, turn off left to Fyfield and Eastleach. Keep left again as the lane splits at **Fyfield**, following the gently rising valley to Eastleach. There are two separately named halves to the village and the lane ends at a junction by the church in **Eastleach Martin**. Go left, and re-cross the Leach to enter

A Highland cow paddling at Coln St Aldwyns

2h30	11.25 MILES	26.9 KM	LEVEL 123

MAP: OS Explorer OL45 The Cotswolds

START/FINISH: Coln St Aldwyns; grid ref: SP 145052

TRAILS/TRACKS: minor lanes

LANDSCAPE: gently rolling Cotswold hills

PUBLIC TOILETS: none on route

TOURIST INFORMATION: Cirencester, tel 01285 654180

CYCLE HIRE: none locally

THE PUB: The Swan at Southrop, Southrop

🛈 Care on the narrow lanes is required

Getting to the start

The small village of Coln St Aldwyns nestles in the Coln Valley some 8 miles (12.9km) east of Cirencester. The nearest town is Fairford on the A417, just over 2 miles (3.2km) to the south along the vale. Park in a cul-de-sac at the centre of the village.

Why do this cycle ride?

Cotswold villages are famed the world over for their quintessential English beauty, but in reality, only a handful have become a fixture of the tourist trail. There are many others, content in their anonymity, which have no less charm, and which offer a quiet escape from hectic modern life. It is through villages such as these that this pleasant ride meanders, crossing the rolling downs between the pretty valleys of the Coln and Leach.

Researched and written by: Dennis Kelsall

Coln St Aldwyns

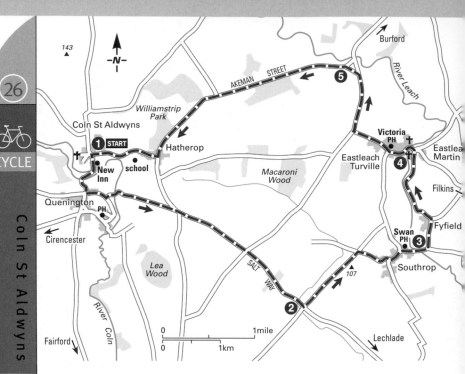

the neighbouring parish, swinging left again beneath a massive **willow tree**, from which a track leads off to **Eastleach Turville's church**.

4 The main lane winds on past the village cross and then a row of **almshouses** to reach a junction below The Victoria pub. Keep ahead, the way signed 'Hatherop and

Burford', climbing shortly to a second junction where you should go right in the direction of **Burford and Westwell**. Undulate onwards across open hills that are interspersed with clumps of copse. Stay left at successive turnings to curve above the higher reaches of the Leach valley, signs now directing you to **Hatherop and Coln St Aldwyns**.

5 For 1.25 miles (2km), the way follows the course of **Akeman Street**, a Roman road, passing a turn off signed to **Dean Farm** before breaking away from line of the ancient thoroughfare into **Hatherop**. At a junction, go right towards Coln St Aldwyns, winding down to leave the village past **Hatherop School**. It is then only a short ride back to the start at Coln St Aldwyns.

A pretty house in Coln St Aldwyns

The Swan at Southrop

The Swan stands at one end of the tiny green in this quintessential Cotswold village, its old stone walls absolutely covered in creepers. This cosy village pub dates back to 1645 and has a mixed history – at one time it was the premises of the local coffin maker. John Keble, the poet and clergyman, frequented the pub when he lived at the Old Vicarage. Today's Swan has been attractively smartened up and, despite offering some classy modern pub food, it successfully retains its pubby charm with a stone-floored locals' bar dispensing pints of Hook Norton, and a well-used skittle alley. Flagstones, open fires and chunky furnishings characterise the low-beamed dining room. Watch the world go by on a summer's day at pavement tables.

Food

Food at The Swan cleverly mixes British and European classics. Menus in the bar offer potted shrimps, goujons of fresh plaice, steak sandwich and home-baked ham, egg and chips alongside linguine carbonara and a plate of Spanish cured meats with pickled chillies. The separate dining room menu offers the likes of confit of duck and foie gras terrine, steak with béarnaise, and pannacotta with poached rhubarb.

Family facilities

Children of all ages are welcome. Small portions from the menus are available and activities (colouring pads) can be provided.

Alternative refreshment stops

In Coln St Aldwyns you'll find the New Inn along the way, or try The Victoria at Eastleach Turville (see Route 31 for details).

☞ Where to go from here

Experience the clack of loom-shuttles and the evocative smell of wood-oil while you watch age-old skills of spinning and weaving transform fleece into woollen fabric at the Cotswold Woollen Weavers at Filkins. Head off into Cirencester to visit the Corinium Museum (www.cotswold.gov.uk), or enjoy the rare and endangered animals, the children's farmyard, and the adventure playground at the Cotswold Wildlife Park near Burford (www.cotswoldwildlifepark.co.uk).

about the pub

The Swan at Southrop
Southrop, Lechlade
Gloucestershire GL7 3NU
Tel: 01367 850205

DIRECTIONS: village signposted off the A361 Lechlade to Burford road, 2 miles (3.2km) north of Lechlade. Pub is located adjacent to the village green.

PARKING: roadside

OPEN: daily

FOOD: daily

BREWERY/COMPANY: free house

REAL ALE: Hook Norton Bitter, Greene King Abbot Ale, Morland Original

Gloucestershire's gardens around Mickleton

A walk that takes you past Kiftsgate Court and Hidcote Manor Garden, two early 20th-century creations of international repute.

Hidcote Manor Garden

Hidcote and Kiftsgate gardens

This walk takes you within striking distance of two of the finest planned gardens in the country. The first, Kiftsgate Court, is the lesser known but nonetheless demands a visit. Its garden was created just after World War One by Heather Muir, a friend of Major Johnson, who created the nearby Hidcote Manor Garden. Kiftsgate's gardens are designed around a hillside overlooking Mickleton and the Vale of Evesham, with terraces, paths, flowerbeds and shrubs. The layout is in the form of rooms and the emphasis is more on the plants themselves, rather than the design.

The second horticultural treat is Hidcote Manor Garden, the fruit of over 40 years of work by Major Lawrence Johnson, an East Coast American who purchased the 17th-century manor house in 1907 and gave it to the National Trust in 1948. Many consider it be one of the greatest of English gardens, and certainly it is one of the most influential. Hidcote grew from almost nothing – when Major Johnson first arrived there was a just a cedar tree and a handful of beeches on 11 acres (4.5ha) of open wold. To some extent it reconciles the formal and informal schools of garden design. Hidcote is not one garden but several. Like Kiftsgate it is laid out in a series of 'outdoor rooms', with walls of stone and hornbeam, yew and box hedge.

The walk begins in Mickleton, at the foot of the Cotswold escarpment, below these two fine gardens. The parish church at the village edge lurks behind a striking house in the so-called Cotswold Queen Anne style. Near the hotel in the village centre is a Victorian memorial fountain designed by William Burges, the architect behind Cardiff Castle. There is also a fine butcher's shop here, a sight to behold, especially in autumn, when it's festooned with locally shot pheasant. As if to further enhance the village's Cotswold credentials, this was also the birthplace of Endymion Porter, a patron of the Cotswold Olimpick Games on Dover's Hill (see page 124).

the walk

1 Of the two footpaths signed at the end of the lane by the **church**, take the one climbing right up a bank to a kissing gate. Cross a meadow on a trod parallel with the right boundary, passing through a gate into thicket. Emerging from the wood at the far side into a field, follow its left margin to a gate. In the next field go half right to leave at the corner.

A fountain in the garden at Kiftsgate Court, created after World War One by Heather Muir

WALK

Mickleton

GLOUCESTERSHIRE

| 2h30 | 4.75 MILES | 7.6 KM | LEVEL 123 |

2 Cross a road and climb to a gate, turning right along the edge of the field. After 250yds (229m), bear right into the adjacent **trees**, which cloak a steep bank falling to the right. Eventually the path leads into a field and on to a **Dutch barn**.

3 Go left and left again onto a track, but immediately turn off right to walk away with a hedge on your right. At the bottom corner of the field, pass through a gap to a **stiled bridge** across a stream.

4 Turn left following the field margin around two corners until you reach a gate. Go left through it and follow a path out to a junction of lanes. Take the one opposite through **Hidcote Boyce**, and where the lane later turns right, continue ahead past **Top Farm**.

5 Beyond a gate, keep going along a rising track for just over 0.25 mile (400m) to pass through another gate into a

MAP: OS Explorer 205 Stratford-upon-Avon & Evesham

START/FINISH: Mickleton: free car park behind parish church; grid ref: SP 162434

PATHS: fields, firm tracks, some possibly muddy woodland, 3 stiles

LANDSCAPE: woodland, open hills and villages

PUBLIC TOILETS: none on route

TOURIST INFORMATION: Moreton-in-Marsh, tel 01608 650881

THE PUB: The Kings Arms, Mickleton

Getting to the start

Mickleton is 8 miles (12.9km) due east of Evesham at the junction of the B4632 and B4081. Park in the small car park behind the parish church.

Researched and written by:
Dennis Kelsall, Christopher Knowles

field. Carry on climbing roughly parallel with the right boundary to the top right corner, passing into an area of grassy mounds. Leave the obvious track to keep left of a **barn**, joining the upper left wall and then exiting through a gate.

6 Carry on at the field edge to come out at a junction and swing sharp left onto a narrow lane leading to **radio masts**. Immediately before the transmitters, turn left onto a track. It winds all the way down the hill, ending at the car park for **Hidcote Manor Garden**. Leave through the exit opposite on to the lane ahead. You can then abandon it almost immediately for a parallel path in the trees, accessed through a small gate on the left. Continue at the edge of the field beyond, returning to the road at the corner.

7 Turn right towards the entrance of **Kiftsgate Court**, but drop through a large gate on the left just before it into

what to look for

In Hidcote Boyce some of the houses, though built of stone broadly in the Cotswold style, are unusually tall. There doesn't seem to be any good reason for this, but the style is almost unique to the village. Climbing the hill out of Hidcote Bartrim, you will find yourself in an area of bumps and hillocks – these are the remains of an old stone quarry.

a sloping meadow. Walk down the valley, passing through trees into the next field. Remaining near the left side, keep descending to leave through a gate at the bottom. Follow the left field margin around the corner, continuing past a footbridge to a gate. Carry on at the edge of the next field and then across a meadow, leaving between **two cemeteries** behind Mickleton's church. To find **The Kings Arms**, go back to High Street, where it stands

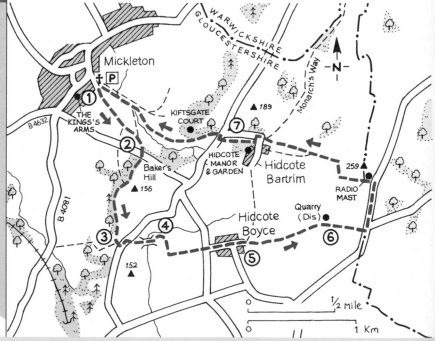

The Kings Arms

As with the two magnificent gardens on this rewarding ramble, the best time to visit The Kings Arms is in the spring and summer for it too has an amazing summer garden – delightful to relax in with a pint of Flowers IPA. Built in 1718 and Grade II listed, this village local has remained largely untouched by modern-day pub developments. Antiques and works of art (with price tags) are displayed throughout the civilised, open-plan lounge and dining room, and many visitors come just to browse the bars. Other than antiques, expect open fires, a welcoming locals' bar with traditional games, and a wide choice of good-value pub food.

Food

From the printed menu choose decent sandwiches (beef fillet slices with caramelised onions and mustard mayonnaise), Stilton ploughman's, chicken, bacon and avocado salad, or the famous Kings burger of the day. Daily specials may include lemon and pepper haddock and roasted lamb shank with rosemary and redcurrant sauce.

Family facilities

Families are welcome. Young children have their own menu and there's a children's play area in the very safe rear garden.

about the pub

The Kings Arms
High Street, Mickleton
Moreton-in-Marsh, Gloucestershire
GL65 6RT
Tel: 01386 438257
www.kings-arms.co.uk

DIRECTIONS: on the High Street (B4081) south of the church
PARKING: 25
OPEN: daily
FOOD: daily
BREWERY/COMPANY: free house
REAL ALE: Flowers Original, IPA & Best
DOGS: allowed in garden only

Alternative refreshment stops

In Mickleton the Butchers Arms serves good pub food, and the Three Ways Hotel is the home of the 'Pudding Club'. There is also a restaurant at Hidcote Manor Garden and a tea room at Kiftsgate Court.

☞ Where to go from here

Don't miss the gardens at Kiftsgate Court and Hidcote Manor Garden (www.nationaltrust.org.uk). Explore nearby Chipping Campden or visit Batsford Arboretum, one of the largest private collections of trees in the country.

From Chipping Campden to Dover's Hill

Walk out from the Cotswolds' most beautiful wool town to Dover's Hill, the site of Whitsuntide festivities.

Cotswold Olimpicks

The Cotswold Olimpicks bear only a passing resemblance to their famous international counterpart. What they lack in grandeur and razzmatazz, however, they make up for in picturesqueness and local passion. Far from being a multi-million dollar shrine to technology which seems so vital to the modern Olympics, the stadium is a natural amphitheatre – the summit of Dover's Hill, on the edge of the Cotswold escarpment.

Dover's Hill is named after the founder of the Cotswold Olimpicks, Robert Dover. Established with the permission of James I, they were dubbed 'royal' games. Dover was born in Norfolk in 1582. His profession brought him to the Cotswolds but he had memories of the plays and spectacles that he had seen in the capital, for this was the era of Shakespeare.

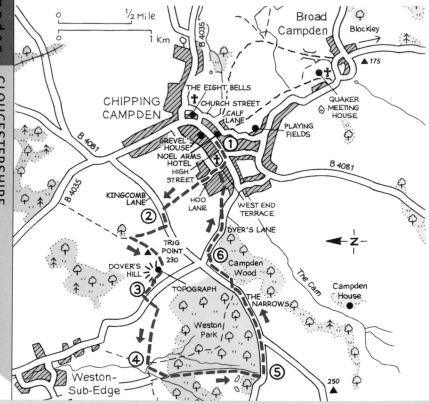

It is generally accepted that the first games took place in 1612, but they may well have begun earlier. Initially the main events were horse-racing and hare-coursing. Other competitions were for running, jumping, throwing, wrestling and staff fighting. The area was festooned with yellow flags and ribbons and there were many dancing events as well as pavilions for chess and other similarly cerebral contests.

Nowadays, the games are a more like a cross between pantomime and carnival, but they have somehow retained their atmosphere of local showmanship. At the end of the events all the spectators, holding flaming torches, file down the road back into Chipping Campden, where the festivities continue with dancing and music along the main street and in the square.

Try to linger in Chipping Campden. A leisurely stroll along its curving High Street of handsome stone houses is essential. The church too is particularly fine and it's also worthwhile searching out the Ernest Wilson Memorial Garden, on the High Street.

| 2h30 | 4.75 MILES | 7.6 KM | LEVEL 1 2 3 |

MAP: OS Explorer OL45 The Cotswolds

START/FINISH: Chipping Campden High Street or main square; grid ref: SP 151391

PATHS: fields, roads and tracks, 7 stiles

LANDSCAPE: open hillside, woodland and village

PUBLIC TOILETS: a short way down Sheep Street

TOURIST INFORMATION: Chipping Campden, tel 01386 841206

THE PUB: The Eight Bells, Chipping Campden

Getting to the start

Chipping Campden, stands midway between Evesham and Moreton-in-Marsh, where the B4081 meets the B4035. Although there is no large car park, you will find plenty of roadside parking in and around the High Street. The walk begins by the medieval market hall on the High Street.

Researched and written by:
Dennis Kelsall, Christopher Knowles

WALK

Chipping Campden

GLOUCESTERSHIRE

the walk

1 From the medieval market hall in the middle of Chipping Campden, walk west along High Street past the Noel Arms Hotel. At **St Catharine's Catholic Church**, turn right into **West End Terrace**, keeping ahead into **Hoo Lane** when it shortly bends right. Carry on up to a farm, but where the track then swings into a field, go forward through a pinch stile on the climbing Cotswold Way, eventually meeting **Kingcomb Lane**.

2 Turn left, then after 50yds (46m), go right on a contained path leading to

Chipping Campden

GLOUCESTERSHIRE

the top of **Dover's Hill**. Walk left along the escarpment, from which there is a splendid view to the west, passing the **trig point** to reach a **topograph**. Now swing right down the grassy slope, ignoring the first stile seen over to the left to find a second one onto a road, about 300yds (274m) from the top.

3 Over a stile opposite, walk away along the bottom of two fields to a kissing gate on the right, concealed in the corner just beyond a **horse shelter**. The way now lies straight down the hillside from field to field, eventually crossing a track to the right of a **cottage**. Carry on ahead to the bottom left corner of the field.

4 Cross the first of the two bridge and stiles that you find there and walk on with a hedge and then a stream to your right. Over another stile and bridge in the far corner, turn left onto a climbing **woodland path**. Entering a field higher up, the way develops as a track, ultimately ending at a country lane.

5 Turn left and then at a junction, go left again onto a busy road, **The Narrows**. Remaining alert to traffic, follow it down for 0.33 mile (500m). Rounding a left-hand bend, look for a waymarked gap on the

what to look for

On reaching Dover's Hill, the route almost doubles back on itself – this is necessary in order to observe legal rights of way. Spend a little time at the topograph – on a clear day there is much to try to identify. In Chipping Campden, look out for the 14th-century Grevel's House, opposite Church Lane. William Grevel, called 'the flower of the wool merchants of all England', is thought to have been the inspiration for the merchant in The Canterbury Tales.

right, through which you can continue on an accompanying field path. After some 400yds (366m), swing half right, cutting the field corner to exit at **Dyer's Lane**.

6 Keep going downhill, shortly passing a cottage on the right. Then, some 100yds (91m) beyond, turn left into a short field access track. Over a stile on the right, walk forward towards the buildings of **Chipping Campden**, emerging onto a street at the far side of the field. Cross to a footpath between the houses opposite, which takes you back onto **West End Terrace**. Turn right and retrace your footsteps to the town centre.

Postal deliveries in Chipping Campden

The Eight Bells

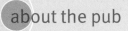

about the pub

The Eight Bells
Church Street, Chipping Campden
Gloucestershire GL55 6JG
Tel: 01386 840371
www.eightbellsinn.co.uk

DIRECTIONS: Church Street is off High Street, just beyond the old market hall	
PARKING: roadside parking	
OPEN: daily; all day Friday, Saturday & Sunday	
FOOD: daily	
BREWERY/COMPANY: free house	
REAL ALE: Hook Norton Best & Old Hooky, guest beer	
DOGS: welcome in the bar and garden	
ROOMS: 4 en suite	

Originally constructed in the 14th century to house the stonemasons and store the bells during construction of the nearby church, this tiny, low-built inn of Cotswold stone has two bars where the original oak beams, open fireplaces and even a priest's hole still survive. For centuries the pub has provided refreshment for the folk of this historic wool and silversmith town. Now, many of the customers are tourists, but traditions are upheld with a range of good local and guest ales and a seasonal menu reflecting a serious approach to food. During the summer the pub is hung with attractive flower baskets, and can be accessed through a cobbled entranceway where the bars lead on to the dining room. There is also an enclosed courtyard for drinking and dining in fine weather, plus terraced gardens overlooking the almshouses and the church.

Food

Freshly prepared local food is offered from a daily changing menu. Options range from salads and light dishes to full Sunday lunch. Typically, tuck into a starter of tomato and basil risotto, followed by seared tuna on niçoise salad with plum tomato oil and pesto, or confit loin of pork with five spice jus, and round off with raspberry Bakewell tart with lavender anglaise. Sandwiches, home-baked ham and chutney, and smoked salmon and scrambled egg are served at lunchtime only.

Family facilities

Children are welcome inside the pub. You'll find a kids menu (with colouring competition) and high chairs, and the rear courtyard and terrace is safe for children.

Alternative refreshment stops

Chipping Campden has plenty of pubs, tea rooms and restaurants. Badgers Hall, on the High Street, does a fine tea.

☛ Where to go from here

Broadway Tower, associated with William Morris, stands about 4 miles (6.4km) to the south west of Chipping Campden. A Gothic folly, built of Portland stone in 1799, it glowers across the Vale of Evesham. There is an interesting small museum inside and fine views across the vale from the top.

Blockley, Batsford and the arboretum

The exotic legacy of a 19th-century diplomat adorns this part of the Cotswold escarpment.

Batsford and Blockley

England seems to be a country of trees – it is a feature that visitors often remark on. Walking through Gloucestershire you are surrounded by many native species but, when you visit Batsford Arboretum, you will encounter 50 acres (20.3ha) of woodland containing over 1,000 species of trees and shrubs from all over the world, particularly from China, Japan and North America.

The arboretum was originally a garden created in the 1880s by the traveller and diplomat, Bertie Mitford, 1st Lord Redesdale, grandfather to the renowned Mitford sisters. Posted as an attaché to the British Embassy in Tokyo, he became deeply influenced by the Far East. Throughout the park there are bronze statues, brought from Japan by Bertie Mitford, and a wide range of bamboos. After the 1st Lord Dulverton purchased Batsford in 1920, his son transformed the garden into the arboretum we see today, with its 90 species of magnolia, maples, cherry trees and conifers, all in a beautiful setting on the Cotswold escarpment. Batsford village is comparatively recent, having grown up at the gates of Batsford Park, a neo-Tudor house built between 1888 and 1892 by Ernest George. George built it for Lord Redesdale to replace an earlier, Georgian house. (It is not open to the public but is clearly visible from the arboretum.) Batsford church was constructed a little before the house, in 1862, in a neo-Norman style. It has several monuments to the Mitford family and a fine work by the sculptor Joseph Nollekens from 1808.

This walk starts in the unspoilt village of Blockley. The village was originally owned by the bishops of Worcester but it didn't really begin to prosper until the 19th century. At one time no fewer than six silk mills, with over 500 employees, were driven by Blockley's fast-flowing stream. Their silks went mostly to Coventry for the production of ribbon. Blockley's history is both enlightened and superstitious. It was one of the first villages in the world to have electric light: in the 1880s Dovedale House was illuminated through Lord Edward Spencer-Churchill's use of water to run a dynamo.

In the early part of that same century the millenarian prophetess, Joanna Southcott, lived in the village until her death in 1814. The tower of Blockley's substantial church predates the silk boom by only 100 years or so, but inside the church are several imposing monuments to the owners of the local mansion, Northwick Park. At least two of these monuments are by the eminent sculptor, John Michael Rysbrack (1694–1770).

the walk

1 With Blockley's church above you to the right, walk south along Lower Street, the B4479, past **Lower Brook House**. Just beyond, turn left onto a lane signed to **Pasture Farm**. Follow it up the hill for 0.25 mile (400m). As you approach a **barn**, bear off right to go behind it.

2 Follow the field edge up, leaving at the top corner onto a **grassy drove** that later widens into a neglected field. Keep going beside the top boundary, eventually passing into a **crop field**. Carry on by the left-hand hedge, maintaining the same direction across the next field as its hedge curves away down the slope.

3 Emerging onto a road, walk left down to a crossroads, there turning right into **Batsford estate village**. At a T-junction, Batsford church lies to the right, while the onward route is left, back to the main road and then right.

4 Leave after some 50yds (46m) along a contained footpath on the right and maintain your direction for 0.5 mile (800m) at the edge of successive fields, which are overlooked by **Batsford House**, set against a curtain of woodland to the west.

Purple aubretia spills out of flower tubs along Blockley High Street

2h15   4.5 MILES   7.2 KM   LEVEL 123

MAP: OS Explorer OL45 The Cotswolds
START/FINISH: Blockley: on edge of churchyard, just off main street; grid ref: SP 165349
PATHS: lanes, tracks and fields, 5 stiles
LANDSCAPE: woodland, hills with good views and villages
PUBLIC TOILETS: on B4479 below Blockley church
TOURIST INFORMATION: Moreton-in-Marsh, tel 01608 650881
THE PUB: The Crown Inn, Blockley

Getting to the start

Blockley lies on the B4479 just north of the A44 Moreton-in-Marsh to Evesham road, 3 miles (4.8km) north west of Moreton-in-Marsh. As there is no convenient car park, park at a safe spot by the roadside on Lower Street below the parish church.

Researched and written by:
Dennis Kelsall, Christopher Knowles

WALK

Blockley

GLOUCESTERSHIRE

5 On reaching a field still bearing the ridges of medieval ploughing, turn right by a **four-fingered waymark** towards a house. Keep ahead across a drive (which leads to Batsford Arboretum) and follow a rising trod to a stile below a wood. Joining a track just above, follow it up for 400yds (366m) to a waymark, there doubling back sharp right. Turn left in front of **gates** into the private park and continue by the estate wall, cresting the hill to meet a lane.

6 Cross to a track opposite, which drops beside a couple of fields. Finding a path in the bottom trees, follow it left through a gate. After 250yds (229m), mount a stile beside another gate on the right and descend the hill along the field edge towards **Blockley**. At the bottom, go over a stile on the right and continue down, crossing **Park Farm's drive** to a stile in the lower right corner. Keep at the edge of the next field and leave along a track out to a lane. Turn right back past Lower Brook House.

what to look for

An unusual feature of Blockley is its raised footpaths, running along the main street. It was noted in the 19th century that 'many dangerous accidents were occurring'. A parish waywarden of the day, Richard Belcher, added iron posts and railings, 'setting the unemployed to work in January and February'. At the south western end of the High Street is Rock Cottage where the prophetess, Joanna Southcott, lived.

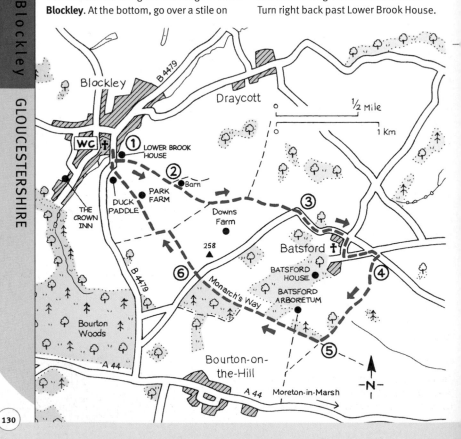

The Crown Inn

Facing the main street, The Crown is a long, low building of honey-coloured Cotswold stone overgrown with creepers, the large arch in the façade immediately declaring its origin as a coaching inn. At street level the inn is fronted by a split-level bar filled with old beams, log fires and exposed stone walls, creating a warm and welcoming atmosphere. Here at any time, and at pavement tables in summer, is a splendid spot to enjoy some consistently tasty bar snacks, plus a pint of Hook Norton ale. Smartly refurbished bedrooms sport exposed timberwork and original beams as well as en suite facilities.

Food

From a varied bar menu choose chicken Caesar salad, fresh cod and chips, beef, mushroom and Guinness pie, ham, egg and chips, ploughman's lunches or salmon and coriander fishcakes with citrus sauce. Puddings include sticky toffee pudding and chocolate fudge cake. Separate restaurant menu and afternoon cream teas.

Family facilities

Children are welcome in the bars where they can order smaller portions of adult dishes; children's menu for younger family members and high chairs are available.

Alternative refreshment stops

Also in Blockley is the Great Western Arms on Station Road.

☞ Where to go from here

Batsford has 55 acres (22ha) of woodland walks. Close to Batsford Park, the Cotswold Falconry gives daily falconry demonstrations

about the pub

The Crown Inn
High Street, Blockley
Moreton-in-Marsh, Gloucestershire
GL56 9EX
Tel: 01386 700245
www.crown-inn-blockley.co.uk

DIRECTIONS: located in the upper part of the village above the church, to the left along High Street

PARKING: 20

OPEN: daily; all day

FOOD: daily

BREWERY/COMPANY: free house

REAL ALE: Hook Norton Bitter, Charles Wells Bombardier

DOGS: welcome inside on a lead

ROOMS: 24 en suite

and eagles, owls and hawks can also be seen here. In Moreton-in-Marsh, the Wellington Aviation Museum is a living memorial to the nearby RAF station (www.wellingtonaviation.org).

Bourton-on-the-Water to Clapton-on-the-Hill

Walk on the wilder side of Bourton-on-the-Water to see its natural regeneration.

Bourton-on-the-Water

Despite Bourton-on-the-Water's popularity the throng is easily left behind by heading eastwards to a chain of redundant gravel pits. In the 1970s these were landscaped and filled with water and fish. Now they have bedded in, they seem to be an integral part of the landscape.

The fish and water acted as magnets for a range of wetland birds. During the spring and summer look out for the little grebe and the great crested grebe, as well as the more familiar moorhens and coots, and mallard and tufted ducks. Wagtails will strut about the water's edge, swans and geese prowl across the water and kingfishers, if you are lucky, streak from bush to reed. Come the autumn and there will be vast numbers of ducks – pintail, shoveler, widgeon and pochard among them – as well as occasional visitors like cormorants. Around the lakes or by the rivers you may also spy dippers and, in the hedgerows, members of the finch family.

In the village listen for birdsong and you will hear some improbable 'visitors'. Bourton-on-the-Water's bird sanctuary houses, among other birds, one of the largest collections of penguins in the world.

Penguins aside, Bourton-on-the-Water has a long history. The edge of the village is bounded by the Roman Fosse Way and many of its buildings are a pleasing mix of medieval, Georgian and Victorian. The village can become very crowded in summer so arrive early enough in the morning and you will find the bridges spanning the Windrush (one of which dates back to 1756) and the narrow streets beyond them highly picturesque. You'll see far fewer visitors in little Clapton-on-the-Hill, which overlooks Bourton. Make the brief detour just before Point 5 to see its handsome green and tiny church.

the walk

1 Opposite the entrance to the main pay-and-display coach and car park in Bourton-on-the-Water, a public footpath leads to a lane in front of the **cemetery**. Follow it right, then where it forks in front of **Cotswold Carp Farm**, bear right and pass through the rightmost of the two gates in front of you.

2 Walk along a grass track between lakes until it curves right. Leave there to go forward over a bridge and stile into a field, exiting onto a road at its far side.

An elegant footbridge across the River Windrush

2h15 — 5 **MILES** — 8 **KM** — **LEVEL** 1 2 3

MAP: OS Explorer OL45 The Cotswolds
START/FINISH: Bourton-on-the-Water:
pay-and-display car park on Station Road;
grid ref: SP 169208
PATHS: track and field, can be muddy and
wet in places, 24 stiles
LANDSCAPE: sweeping valley views, lakes,
streams, hills and village
PUBLIC TOILETS: at car park
TOURIST INFORMATION: Bourton-on-the-
Water, tel 01451 820211
THE PUB: The Kingsbridge Inn,
Bourton-on-the-Water

Getting to the start

Bourton-on-the-Water stands beside the
A429, 15 miles (24.1km) north east of
Cirencester. The walk begins from the well-
signed main coach and car park on Station
Road. Alternative parking is on Rissington
Road on the eastern edge of the town.

Researched and written by:
Dennis Kelsall, Christopher Knowles

3 Turn right and then left on to a track to
Santhill Fishery. After 100yds (91m), in
front of a gate, dog-leg over a stile into the
field on the left, following the hedge on
beside the track. Return to the track at the
far end of the field, but where it later turns
through a gate into the fishery, walk
forward across a bridge and immediately
swing left through a kissing gate onto a
wooded path beside the **River Windrush**.
Emerging into a field at the far end, turn
left to a kissing gate and go over a bridge
before turning right beside a lake.

4 About 100yds (91m) beyond a gate,
where a second, smaller lake ends,
bear right to a stile. Wind through trees,
eventually crossing a bridge into a field.
Follow the boundary right to meet a track at
the far side of the next field. Walk forward
along it, but at a junction of tracks by the
entrance to a **house**, carry on ahead to the

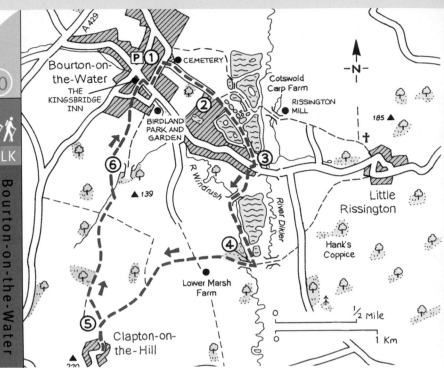

corner. In the next field, after 25yds (23m) dog-leg over a stile to continue on the opposite side of the hedge. Cross another stile and bear slightly left across the next two fields to a stile, then follow the right margin up to a junction of tracks.

5 To the left is the pretty village of **Clapton-on-the-Hill**. In the simple church is an intriguing Latin inscription beside the chancel arch describing an incantation for relief from purgatory. Return to this junction to follow the track in its opposite direction towards Bourton. Entering a field, the Right of Way initially hugs the left hedge then, half way along, crosses to the bottom corner. A grass track then takes you on past a wood before ending in a field at the bottom of the hill. Strike a shallow diagonal to a stile at the far side, maintaining the same course across successive fields until you approach a **wood**.

6 Do not follow the path ahead into the trees, instead, drop to the left, cross a stream and immediately turn right. Keep the same general line, crossing from field to field and eventually you will emerge onto a street at the edge of **Bourton**. Go to the end, turning left and then right into the town centre. After crossing the river beside **The Kingsbridge Inn**, turn right and then left to return to the car park.

what to look for

In the autumn, in particular, keep an eye out for swans. Mute swans – the most common type, with the orange bill – are present all the year round, but the whooper swan, with its erect neck and yellow bill, is only a winter visitor, flying in from northern Europe and Russia.

The Kingsbridge Inn

The Kingsbridge Inn occupies a prime position in this honey-pot tourist village, famously known as the 'Venice of the Cotswolds', as it stands beside one of the many small bridges that span the tranquil River Windrush. Its bench-filled riverside garden and patio bustles with drinkers and diners on fine sunny days. If the weather's poor, the lively, open-plan, waterside bar is the place to be for good real ale and an extensive range of traditional pub food. Equally, the well-equipped en suite bedrooms are popular due to its central location.

Food

Diverse menu choices include cod in home-made beer batter, guinea fowl with chicken and cranberry mousse, daily pies, curries, steaks and roast lunches plus filled baguettes.

Family facilities

Expect a warm welcome towards children as well as a children's menu, high chairs, baby-changing facilities, and a courtyard garden for summer eating and drinking.

Alternative refreshment stops

Bourton-on-the-Water has many pubs, tea shops and restaurants, catering to most tastes. You could also try the Mousetrap on Lansdowne for reliable pub food and the Old Manse, also close to the river, serves a good lunch and dinner.

☛ Where to go from here

Bourton-on-the-Water has many and diverse attractions jostling for the contents of your wallet. The pick of these are probably Birdland Park and Gardens with their penguins, and the Cotswold Motor Museum (www.cotswold-motor-museum.com), which has lots of pre-1950 cars as well as a few novelty items to thrill children. The most popular activity is arguably just strolling around.

about the pub

The Kingsbridge Inn
Riverside, Bourton-on-the-Water
Gloucestershire GL54 2BS
Tel: 01451 820286
www.roomattheinn.info

DIRECTIONS:	beside the River Windrush in the village centre
PARKING:	15
OPEN:	daily; all day
FOOD:	no food Sunday evening
BREWERY/COMPANY:	Eldridge Pope
REAL ALE:	Caledonian Deuchars IPA, Bass, Courage Best
DOGS:	allowed in the bar only
ROOMS:	24 en suite

The Eastleaches and a circuit beyond

Two churches, just a stone's throw apart across a narrow stream.

Anglo-Saxon kingdoms

These two Cotswold villages, sitting cheek by jowl in a secluded valley, carry an air of quiet perfection. Yet Eastleach Turville and Eastleach Martin are quite distinctive, and each has a parish church (though one is now redundant). St Andrews in Eastleach Turville faces St Michael and St Martin's across the narrow River Leach. Their origins lie in the development of the parish system from the early days of the Anglo-Saxon church.

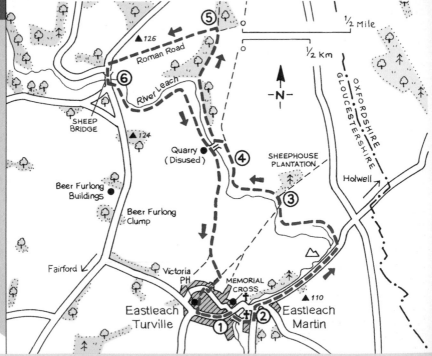

2h00 — **4.5 MILES** — **7.2 KM** — **LEVEL 1**23

MAP: OS Explorer OL45 The Cotswolds

START/FINISH: Eastleach Turville: the Victoria pub car park (let them know you are there); grid ref: SP 198053

PATHS: tracks and lanes, valley paths and woodland, 4 stiles

LANDSCAPE: villages, open wold, narrow valley and streams

PUBLIC TOILETS: none on route

TOURIST INFORMATION: Burford, tel 01993 823558

THE PUB: The Victoria, Eastleach Turville

Getting to the start

Eastleach Turville is located and signposted west of the A361 midway between Burford and Lechlade. Several narrow lanes wind their way to the village and The Victoria pub which stands at the junction where a lane enters from Southrop.

Researched and written by:
Dennis Kelsall, Christopher Knowles

The English parish has its origins in the shifting rivalries of Saxon England; for the one thing that united the various Saxon kingdoms was the Church. The first 'parishes' were really the Anglo-Saxon kingdoms. Christianity, the new power in the land, not only saved souls but also secured alliances. The pope's aim was to invest more bishops to act as pastors and proselytisers, but at the same time their appointments were useful politically. Over the centuries the assorted conventions and appointments that had accumulated through usage coalesced into a hierarchical English Church. Rulers and landholders were influential in the development of the parish system, but many parishes also derived from the gradual disintegration of the local 'minster', a central church on consecrated ground which controlled a group of client chapels. As population and congregations grew, the chapels themselves became new parish churches, with rights equal to those of the minster.

The Norman church of St Michael and St Martin at Eastleach Martin

With the establishment of a single English kingdom, the idea of a parish had diminished geographically to something like modern size. By the 10th century the parish had become the framework for the enforcement of the payment of tithes, the medieval equivalent of an income tax. By the 12th century much of the modern diocesan map of England was established. So in the Eastleaches, all these developments come together and you find two parish churches virtually side by side. With politics, power and bureaucracy all playing a part, it's likely that the pastoral needs of the community were a long way down the list of factors which led to their creation.

the walk

1 Walk down from **The Victoria** to the main lane below the pub and turn left through Eastleach Turville. Very soon after passing the memorial cross in the village, go right to cross a clapper bridge spanning the River Leach. Follow a path through the **churchyard** of Eastleach Martin to emerge onto a lane.

2 Turn left to a junction, and there go right taking the lower of the two roads, which is signed **Holwell**. Walk on for almost 0.5 mile (800m) to where the road begins to rise steeply, there leaving through a gate on the left. A grass track winds along the valley for another 0.5 mile (800m) to **Sheephouse Plantation**.

A rhino in the Cotswold Wildlife Park which is near Burford

what to look for

The little clapper bridge linking the two parishes is known locally as Keble's Bridge, after a family which was eminent in the area. John Keble, after whom Keble College in Oxford is named, was nominal curate for the two parishes in the 19th century. In the middle part of the walk the straight track to a road is part of Akeman Street, the Roman road that linked Cirencester with St Albans.

3 Through a gate into the next field, walk on with the trees on your right. Ignore a gate beyond them and carry on beside a **wall**. Where the wall ends, cross a stile to continue your line in the adjacent field.

4 Keep ahead from field to field, shortly going by a gated bridge spanning the river over to your left. Now, bear left, passing below a lone copper beech to find a **gate** at the bottom corner of a wood. A path winds on through the trees, meeting a crossing track after 0.5 mile (800m).

5 Turn left here and follow it out of the woods, continuing between the fields beyond, and eventually emerging onto a lane. Turn left down to **Sheep Bridge** and, just before a junction, go into the field on the left.

6 A meandering path follows the valley bottom, occasional yellow topped **marker posts** indicating the Right of Way. Keep on through gates, eventually reaching the gated bridge passed earlier in the day. There, leave the valley floor, rising gently beside the right-hand wall to a gate. Carry on along a track. However, in the next field veer left to leave by a gate in the far wall. Walk ahead to reach a lane beside the **village hall**. Go right, but then almost immediately left along a footpath, which leads back to The Victoria.

The Victoria

about the pub

The Victoria
Eastleach Turville, Fairford
Gloucestershire GL7 3NQ
Tel: 01367 850277

DIRECTIONS: see Getting to the Start
PARKING: 30
OPEN: daily
FOOD: daily
BREWERY/COMPANY: Arkells Brewery
REAL ALE: Arkells BBB, Kingsdown &
seasonal ale
DOGS: allowed in the bar and garden

Prints of Her Majesty keep an eye on things here, though The Victoria has been a pub since the 18th century, long before she came to the throne, and the building itself is over 500 years old. This small, stone-built country pub enjoys a quiet and tranquil setting, with a terrace and lawned front garden overlooking the mellowed Cotswold village. Inside, too, the atmosphere is relaxed and unassuming, with plenty of character from low oak beams, a crackling log fire in the stone fireplace, and simple furnishings throughout the unspoiled rooms that ramble around the central bar. Add tip-top local Arkells beer on hand-pump and good home-made bar meals, freshly prepared using local and organic seasonal produce and you have a splendid, traditional country local to retreat to after your walk.

Food

Menus change daily; at lunch there may be organic pork and leek sausages, Gruyère and asparagus tartlet on dressed leaves, warm chicken, bacon and Brie salad, and calves liver, smoked bacon and red wine sauce, alongside filled baguettes. Evening additions include lamb shanks, steaks and fresh fish.

Family facilities

There are no special facilities for children but they are allowed in the eating areas of the bar and the dining room. Good, safe garden for fine sunny days.

Alternative refreshment stops

There are no other refreshment stops on this walk. There is, however, a restaurant serving hot and cold meals and snacks at the Cotswold Wildlife Park.

☞ Where to go from here

Visit the Cotswold Wildlife Park and Gardens near Burford (www.cotswoldwildlifepark.co.uk). Take a stroll around the picture-postcard village of Bibury to see the stone cottages at Arlington Row, and visit the working Bibury Trout Farm where children can feed the fish and try to catch a trout.

Adlestrop to Lower Oddington

Embracing the legacies of Warren Hastings and the poet Edward Thomas.

Daylesford

Warren Hastings' role in the making of the British Empire, was paramount. Born in the nearby village of Churchill, Hastings joined the East India Company and by 1773 was Governor-General of Bengal. That India became the fulcrum of the British Empire was largely due to his work. Upon his return to England, he purchased Daylesford, lost earlier by his family, where he died in 1818. Daylesford House was rebuilt to the design of the architect Samuel Cockerell. The building is in the Classical style with Moorish features. The parkland around Daylesford House was laid out in 1787 by the landscape gardener Humphrey Repton in the spacious style of the day.

Daylesford grew up to house the workers who helped to make the estate profitable. Similarly, Daylesford church was rebuilt by Hastings in 1816 as a place of worship for the estate workers. By 1860 the congregation had outgrown the church, so it was redesigned. Warren Hastings' tomb lies outside the east window.

If Hastings represents the British Empire at its strongest then, in Adlestrop, you will find echoes of the changing world which signalled its decline. This small village has become associated with one of the best-known poems in English, written by the war poet, Edward Thomas (1878–1917). Called simply 'Adlestrop', the poem captures a single moment as a train halts briefly at the village's station with its haunting evocation of the drowsy silence of a hot summer day. You'll find the old station sign now decorates a bus shelter and the old station bench has the poem inscribed upon it.

the walk

1 From the car park, turn left along the road, passing a junction where a bus shelter sports the old Adlestrop railway station sign. Some 200yds (183m) after the next junction, leave across a stile on the right to follow a **woodland path** paralleling the lane. Continue on this path until it eventually ends over a stile at a main road.

2 Cross with care and turn left along the verge. Immediately before reaching a lane to Cornwell, turn right through a gate onto a path into the **Daylesford Estate**. Approaching a fence it curves left beside it, shortly reaching a junction. The Right of Way continues through a gate in front of you, dropping diagonally across a **paddock**, but if horses are there, skirt around it along the contained grass track to the right. Emerging from the paddock at the far corner, walk forward on a fenced grass track between more enclosures.

3 Over a bridge, follow a tree-lined avenue, crossing a drive to reach a **stable yard**. Walk through to the far side and then turn right, passing the **estate office** towards the gardens.

4 Continue down beyond paddocks and later, the entrance to the garden offices. At a fork a little further on, go right to remain on the **main drive**, which eventually leads out to a lane.

2h15 **5.25 MILES** **8.4 KM** **LEVEL 123**

5 Turn right and follow the road until you reach a junction into the Daylesford estate village. Just beyond, on the left, a shaded footpath leads to **Daylesford Church**, the key to which is available from the Cottage or the Old Rectory. After looking around, return to the road and retrace your steps past the junction, looking for a **waymarked kissing gate** about 100yds (91m) further along on the right.

6 Follow the field edge to a **footbridge** spanning the railway and join a winding track across a stream towards a field access bridge. Use the gated pedestrian bridge beside it, rejoining the track which curves to leave the far right corner of the field. At that point, however, the Right of Way passes into the adjacent field through the hedge on the right to climb parallel with the track. Instead of rejoining the track higher up, walk forward into the next field and accompany the hedge away to the right. Go left at the corner to remain in the same field, leaving just beyond the top corner onto a track.

7 Turn right, passing **Oddington Church** and shortly emerging at a junction in the village. Go right to find **The Fox** inn and continue to the main road. Walk right along the pavement, first on this side and then on the other, crossing the carriageway carefully, for traffic moves quickly.

Right: A track near Lower Oddington
Next page: The church at Lower Oddington

MAP: OS Explorer OL45 The Cotswolds

START/FINISH: Adlestrop: Car park (donations requested) outside village hall; grid ref: SP 241272

PATHS: track, field and road, 2 stiles

LANDSCAPE: rolling fields, woodland and villages

PUBLIC TOILETS: none on route

TOURIST INFORMATION: Stow-on-the-Wold, tel 01451 831082

THE PUB: The Fox, Lower Oddington

Getting to the start
Adlestrop lies just north of the A436, 3 miles (4.8km) east of Stow-on-the-Wold. Leave your car in a small car park in front of the village hall, from where the walk begins.

Researched and written by:
Dennis Kelsall, Christopher Knowles

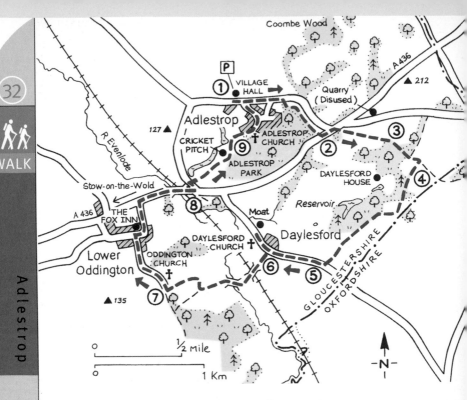

8 A short distance after the **railway bridge**, turn off left towards Adlestrop. However, almost immediately leave through consecutive kissing gates on the right into Adlestrop Park. Strike out, joining a track towards the far side that skirts the village **cricket green** to a gate.

9 Keep going past **Adlestrop Church** and then turn left when you reach a junction. Carry on through the village, soon returning to the bus shelter near the car park.

what to look for

As you walk around Daylesford Park, try to catch a glimpse of the house – it's almost impossible as it's very cleverly concealed behind ornamental parkland. This, it seems, was a deliberate ruse, fashionable in the 18th century, to preserve privacy whilst creating a harmonious landscape in keeping with the surrounding countryside. In Adlestrop, look out for the site of the old station, immortalised by Edward Thomas in his poetry.

The Fox

about the pub

The Fox
Lower Oddington, Stow-on-the-Wold
Gloucestershire GL56 oUR
Tel: 01451 870555
www.foxinn.net

DIRECTIONS: village signposted off A436
east of Stow-on-the-Wold. Pub on main
village street in Lower Oddington close to
the lane leading to the church

PARKING: 15

OPEN: daily; all day

FOOD: no food Sunday evening
October–March

BREWERY/COMPANY: free house

DOGS: allowed in bar and garden only

ROOMS: 3 en suite

*The Fox benefits from one of the most
idyllic and unspoiled village locations in
the Cotswolds, famed for its picture-book
stone cottages and its 11th-century
church of St Nicholas. The inn's 16th-
century, mellow stone façade is largely
hidden by dense Virginia creeper, while
inside are polished slate floors, fresh
flowers and candles on pine tables,
tasteful prints on rag-washed walls, a
blazing log fire in the convivial bar and
daily papers. A cross between a country
brasserie and village pub, it draws the
crowds for its well-kept beers, fine wines,
good, imaginative food, the three tasteful
bedrooms, and the warm, efficient and
friendly service. Super awning-covered,
heated terrace and a pretty, traditional
cottage garden for summer sipping.*

Food
The menu takes advantage of the seasons
and changes regularly. From warm salads,
lasagne and steak and kidney pie, there are
starters/light snacks like venison terrine
with fig and red onion chutney, and
courgette and Stilton risotto, alongside
lamb shank with whole garlic and
rosemary, or seared scallops with rocket
and ginger dressing. Booking is
recommended for Sunday's rare roast beef.

Family facilities
Children of all ages are welcome inside
and smaller portions of main menu dishes
are served. Safe walled garden and patio.

Alternative refreshment stops
Nearby is the Horse and Groom in the
sibling village of Upper Oddington. Stow-
on-the-Wold has many and varied pubs,
restaurants and tea rooms.

☛ Where to go from here
You can visit the handsome Jacobean manor
house at Chastleton with its fine topiary
gardens (www.nationaltrust.org.uk). Stow-
on-the-Wold's Toy and Collector's Museum
(www.thetoymuseum.co.uk) will delight
children, and probably adults too.

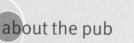

WALK

32

Adlestrop

GLOUCESTERSHIRE

From Todenham to the Ditchfords

Todenham · GLOUCESTERSHIRE

A walk among the ghosts of communities abandoned since the 15th century.

Lost Village

There are cases of so-called 'lost villages' all over England. The principal culprit is often said to be the Black Death, sweeping through the countryside in the 14th century. However, this is by no means the only possibility and in the case of the Ditchfords there do appear to be other reasons for their disappearance. A priest called John

Rouse wrote in 1491 that the Ditchfords had been abandoned during his lifetime. Changes in agricultural practices are thought to be the main reason. As farming became more efficient there was less need to cultivate the stony soils of the more exposed upland areas. In the Cotswolds, the wool trade was rapidly supplanting arable farming. The result was that the villagers, mostly farm labourers who had for centuries depended on access to arable land for their livelihood, lost that access. They simply had to move elsewhere in search of work. Today there are no solid

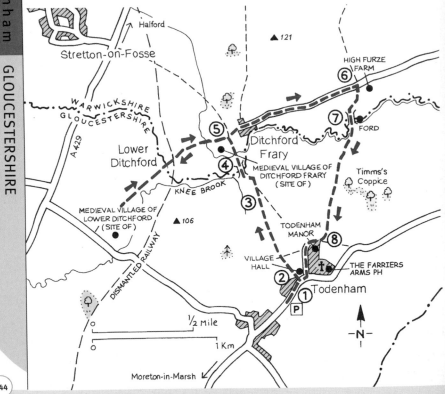

what to look for

As you're crossing the fields at the start of the walk, look for the pleats in the fields that indicate medieval ridge and furrow ploughing techniques. These are common all over central England, though many have been ploughed out by modern machinery. The furrows were created by ox-drawn ploughs, the ridges separated different farmers' workings in the same open field. Each furrow would have been about a furlong (220yds/201m) in length, the distance being about as far as the ploughing beast could pull before it needed a rest.

2h00 · **4.25 MILES** · **6.8 KM** · **LEVEL 123**

MAP: OS Explorer OL45 The Cotswolds

START/FINISH: Todenham: lay-by on main street, south of village hall; grid ref: SP 240360

PATHS: track and field, quiet lanes, ford or bridge, 2 stiles

LANDSCAPE: rolling fields, with good views at some points

PUBLIC TOILETS: none on route

TOURIST INFORMATION: Moreton-in-Marsh, tel 01608 650881

THE PUB: The Farriers Arms, Todenham

Getting to the start

Todenham lies 3 miles (4.8km) north east of Moreton-in-Marsh, reached along a minor lane leaving the A429 on the edge of town. A lay-by in front of a shelter on the right as you enter the village offers convenient parking.

Researched and written by:
Dennis Kelsall, Christopher Knowles

WALK

Todenham GLOUCESTERSHIRE

remains of any of the three villages. What you can see, however, is a series of regular rolls and shapes in the land that indicate settlement. Upper Ditchford, which stood on the slope near Neighbrook Farm, is the least obvious but you can see banked enclosures and terraces. In the case of Lower Ditchford, there are terraces and the site of a manor house and moat. Ditchford Frary has left its name to a farmhouse.

Todenham survived depopluation, and today is a quiet, unspoilt village on the edge of the Cotswolds. It's really a long, single road flanked by an assortment of houses. The manor house dates from the end of the Georgian period whilst the church is worth a visit for its decorated and Perpendicular interior. Its features include a 13th-century font with the names of 18th-century churchwardens inscribed upon it.

the walk

1 From the lay-by, walk up towards the centre of the village. Rounding a bend immediately before Todenham's **village hall,** turn sharp left into the forecourt of a house. Go through a gate to its right to find a track.

2 After a few paces, climb right to a kissing gate and head straight out

Todenham village

across ridged fields, eventually joining a hedge on your right in the third enclosure. Keep ahead where it ends, aiming towards a **large house** visible in the middle distance.

3 Rejoining the right boundary part-way down the next field, keep going over a stile, but towards the bottom, swing half left towards a **derelict brick barn**. To its right, a path drops behind through long grass amidst willow trees, leading to a gated bridge across **Knee Brook**.

4 Over the bridge, walk across an old meadow (the site of the abandoned village of Ditchford Frary), bearing just left of the **farmhouse** ahead to reach a gate. Carry on at the edge of the next field, leaving at its corner onto a **farm track**.

5 The remains of another medieval village, Lower Ditchford lie 0.75 mile (1.2km) along the lane to the left, evident as bumps and hollows in the left-hand field as you approach a lane. Retrace your steps

to this point to continue the walk. Follow the track in the other direction past **Ditchford Frary Farm**, beyond which it is metalled.

6 After 0.75 mile (1.2km) and just before reaching **High Furze Farm** turn right through a gate and follow the field edge down. Approaching the bottom, veer to the right corner, where a footbridge takes you back across **Knee Brook**.

7 Climb away, joining a faint grass track from the ford, just downstream of the **footbridge**, to find a gate in the top right corner. A track rises through a long strip of rough woodland, and although initially sometimes muddy, it becomes firmer on the higher ground. It terminates at a junction of tracks outside an entrance to **Todenham Manor**.

8 To the right, a grass path skirts the manor grounds, finally returning you to the lane beside the village hall.

The Farriers Arms

Tucked away in a sleepy village north of Moreton-in-Marsh, the brick-built Farriers pre-dates 1650 when part of the building was used by the monks who constructed the parish church. As its name suggests, the other part of the building was used as a forge. First mentioned as a pub in 1830, it has changed little over the years, retaining an unspoiled charm with old polished flagstone floors, exposed stone walls, hop-strewn beams, and a huge inglenook with wood-burning stove. Books and old photographs fill an intimate little side room. You'll also find pub games, local micro-brewery guest beers, home-cooked pub food, and tables on a sunny terrace with views of the church.

about the pub

The Farriers Arms
Todenham, Moreton-in-Marsh
Gloucestershire GL56 9PF
Tel: 01608 650901
www.farriersarms.com

DIRECTIONS: turn left from the village hall; pub just beyond the church.

PARKING: 15

OPEN: daily

FOOD: daily

BREWERY/COMPANY: free house

REAL ALE: Hook Norton Bitter, 2 guest beers

DOGS: allowed in the bar and library room on a lead

WALK

Todenham

GLOUCESTERSHIRE

Food

On the snack menu you'll find soup and sandwiches, ploughman's lunches and favourites like ham, egg and chips and steak and kidney pie. The main menu and daily blackboard specials take in pheasant and bacon terrine, whole lemon sole, pork fillet with Stilton sauce, beer-battered cod and chips, and apricot and almond tart.

Family facilities

Well-behaved children are welcome in the restaurant or library room. There's a children's menu as well as books and colouring equipment to keep them amused.

Alternative refreshment stops

None on the route. The market town of Moreton-in-Marsh, 3 miles (4.8km) south west, has plenty of pubs, cafés, and restaurants.

☛ Where to go from here

Both Moreton-in-Marsh and Stow-on-the-Wold are charming small Cotswold towns and worth strolling around. In autumn, head for Batsford Arboretum (www.batsarb.co.uk) to experience the magnificent display of colours, or visit the Cotswold Falconry Centre for falconry demonstrations.

Burford and the Windrush Valley

Discover ancient village churches, built by master craftsmen from stone that was later used in Westminster Abbey.

Windrush Valley churches

The wealth generated by medieval sheep farming is evident in Burford's church, a magnificent edifice topped by a soaring spire, which is said to be one of the highest in Oxfordshire. Yet although the surrounding churches may be more modest in scale, they each have qualities worthy of investigation. At Little Barrington there is magnificent Norman stonework around the doorway, whilst Great Barrington's church contains an Elizabethan effigy of a Captain Bray, unusually depicting the sword on the right. Pardoned by his queen for killing a man in anger, Bray swore never again to draw his sword with his right hand. The church at Taynton has fine carving decorating the door and windows, with corbels fashioned into heads overlooking the nave. The font, too, is remarkable, adorned with angels, evangelists, and other figures including a mermaid.

At Swinbrook you will find two splendid Tudor-style monuments and the graves of Nancy, Unity and Pamela Mitford, whose family held Asthall Manor. Nancy is known for her novels, which included *Love in a Cold Climate* and Unity gained notoriety because of her association with leading Nazis. At St Nicholas's, Asthall, you can see one of the few surviving 'blacksmith' clocks. Widford's church is reached by a footpath off on the right after crossing the

river by Widford Mill. Isolated after the village was abandoned to escape the plague, its walls have sombre 14th-century frescoes, grimly reminding man of his mortality. The building occupies the site of a Roman villa, but a famous tessellated floor, discovered beneath the chancel, is sadly now covered to prevent vandalism.

the ride

1 Riding out of the car park, turn left up Guildenford and then, opposite the **Royal Oak**, go right along Witney Street. At the busy crossroads in the centre of town, cross diagonally into Sheep Street and head past the **hospital** out of the village. After 0.5 mile (800m), just as the road begins to climb, look for a very narrow, unsigned lane leaving on the right. It gently rises and falls along the side of the Windrush Valley, offering picturesque views over the low-lying meadows bordering the river. Although poorly surfaced initially, the lane improves towards **Little Barrington**, passing the village's tiny church along the way.

2 At the end of the lane, drop right beside the green, shortly going right again over the river towards Great Barrington. Beyond **The Fox Inn**, a second bridge heralds a short, but steepish pull into Great Barrington, passing the entrances to **Barrington Park** and the nearby church at the top on your left. Carry on into the village and keep right in front of the **war memorial** for Taynton, the way tracing long undulations along the valley side. The area is famed for its fine stone and the masons who worked it. **Taynton** provided stone for the repair of Westminster Abbey and the

Strong family from Barrington served as master masons for the building of Wren's St Paul's.

3 At Taynton, the **church** is set back from the lane on the right. It was once part of a small monastery belonging to the French abbey of St Denis, which was dissolved by Edward IV and given to the Abbot of Tewkesbury. Cycle through the hamlet and keep ahead towards Burford, eventually reaching a junction with the A424.

4 At this point you can shorten the ride by going forward and then right at a mini roundabout to return to Burford. Otherwise head left up the hill for 200yds (183m) before turning right on a narrow lane. It winds past **Manor Farm** over Westhall Hill, then falls beyond to join the A361. Follow it left through **Fulbrook**, very soon leaving at the second of two turnings on the right, a single track lane signed to Swinbrook. It climbs steadily away between fields and past woodland, later dipping to cross the head of **Dean Bottom** before descending to a junction. **Swinbrook** lies to the right, where another church on the right, St Mary's, merits a visit.

5 Carry on beyond the church for another 200yds (183m) before turning left uphill to leave the village. Keep right with the main lane, still gaining height along the valley side. Later levelling to a junction, go right to **Asthall**, dropping to cross the base of the flat valley where a sporadic line of pollarded willows marks the course of the river. Follow

3h00 — **13.5 MILES** — **21.7 KM** — **LEVEL 1 2 3**

34

CYCLE

Windrush Valley

OXFORDSHIRE/GLOUCESTERSHIRE

MAP: OS Explorer OL45 The Cotswolds
START/FINISH: car park in Burford; grid ref: SP 253122
TRAILS/TRACKS: unclassified country roads and lanes, two short sections on main roads
LANDSCAPE: rolling countryside bordering the River Windrush
PUBLIC TOILETS: at car park
TOURIST INFORMATION: Burford, tel 01993 823558
CYCLE HIRE: none locally
THE PUB: The Fox Inn, Great Barrington
❗ Care to be taken crossing main road in Burford and on two stretches of main road later in ride. The ride is undulating.

Getting to the start
Burford stands by a crossroads of the A40 between Oxford – 23 miles (37km) and Cheltenham – 20 miles (32.2km) and the A361 north from Swindon. A car park, from which the ride begins, is signed along Church Lane from the A361 in the town centre.

Why do this cycle ride?
The ancient wool town of Burford is an attractive focal point for this exploration of the secluded Windrush Valley, presented here as an 'unclosed' figure-of-eight circuit that allows two shorter rides. Surrounded by the rolling Cotswold hills, the Valley is lined with pretty small villages.

Researched and written by: Dennis Kelsall

the lane around right into the village, winding left in front of the church before turning right by the entrance of the **manor**.

6 Head away along the lane to a crossroads, where to the right, just across the river, you will find a welcoming pub, **The Swan Inn**. The onward way, however lies straight over, along the pretty valley, through the tiny hamlet of **Widford** and eventually back to Burford.

Great Barrington

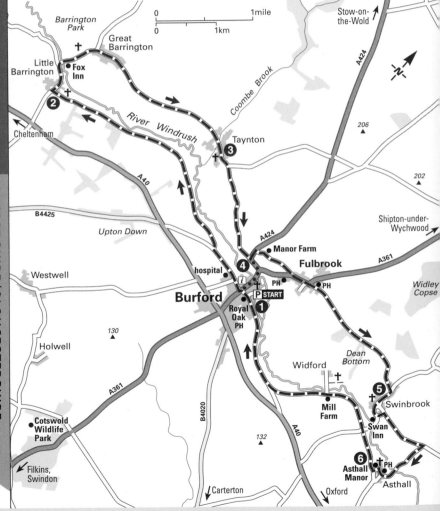

The Fox Inn

about the pub

The Fox Inn
Great Barrington, Burford
Gloucestershire OX18 4TB
Tel: 01451 844385
www.foxinnbarrington.co.uk

DIRECTIONS: The village is signposted off the A40 3 miles (4.8km) west of Burford and the pub is located beside the River Windrush
PARKING: 60
OPEN: daily; all day
FOOD: daily
BREWERY/COMPANY: Donnington Brewery
REAL ALE: Donnington BB & SBA
ROOMS: 4 en suite

A genuinely unspoiled little Cotswold pub, built in the 17th century with the local honey-coloured stone and picturesquely set beside the gently meandering River Windrush. Its charm is of the simple alehouse sort, with low ceilings, stone walls, rustic furnishings, blazing winter log fires, and time-honoured pub games in the small main bar. Modern-day trends do exist here – the former skittle alley now houses a restaurant with river views and a splendid wall mural of the pretty valley, and four comfortable en suite rooms. Lovely river and lakeside gardens and a heated rear terrace make The Fox a great summer pub, in fact the best summer watering-hole for miles. Added attractions include the excellent local Donnington beer, heady farm ciders, and good, home-made food.

Food

Separate lunch and dinner menus offer a varied choice of meals. From lunchtime sandwiches and traditional dishes such as battered cod and chips, home-cooked ham, egg and chips, and beef and ale pie, blackboards may list Thai-style tuna, spinach, leek and chestnut pie, salmon fishcakes, and seasonal game, perhaps pigeon breast casseroled with mushrooms and red wine.

Family facilities

A genuine warm welcome awaits children who will enjoy the splendid lake and riverside gardens (care and supervision required). Inside, there are high chairs and smaller portions of adult dishes are served.

Alternative refreshment stops

You are spoilt for choice in Burford. Take your pick from hotel restaurants, pubs and tea rooms. Along the route there's the Carpenter's Arms and Mason's Arms in Fulbrook, The Swan at Swinbrook (see Route 35), and the Maytime Inn at Asthall.

☛ Where to go from here

The Cotswold Wildlife Park and Gardens (www.cotswoldwildlifepark.co.uk) is a great venue for gardeners and their children, with rare and endangered species in parkland and gardens, and there's a narrow gauge railway and an adventure playground. Learn more about the skills of spinning and weaving woollen fabric at the Cotswold Woollen Weavers in Filkins.

Burford – a classic Cotswold town

Discover the delights of an ancient settlement on this attractive walk through the Windrush Valley.

Gateway to the Cotswolds

Often described as the gateway to the Cotswolds, the picturesque town of Burford has changed little over the years. The High Street runs down between lime trees and mellow stone houses to a narrow three-arched bridge over the River Windrush. Charles II and his mistress Nell Gwynn, whose child was named the Earl of Burford, attended Burford races and stayed at the George Hotel. When she retired to Windsor, Gwynn named her home Burford House.

Burford has always been regarded as an important trading centre. People would pay their tolls at the twin-gabled 15th-century Tolsey, now a museum, for the right to trade in the town and it was here that the prosperous Guild of Merchants conducted their meetings. Take a leisurely stroll through the town and you'll stumble across a host of treasures – especially in the little side roads leading off the High Street. For example, the Great House in Witney Street was the largest residence in Burford when it was built about 1690. With its Georgian façade, it dwarfs the other buildings in the street. The Dolls' House, from 1939 and on view in the Tolsey Museum, is modelled on the Great House.

Burford's parish church, with its slender spire, is one of the largest in Oxfordshire. Begun about 1170, it was enlarged over subsequent centuries and one of its last additions was the south porch, noted for its elaborate stonework. The west doorway is pure Norman, as is the

The High Street in Burford

central part of the tower, to which another stage was added in the 15th century to provide a base for the spire. Inside, the ceiling is fan vaulted and there are five medieval screens dividing various chapels.

The Priory in Priory Lane is another of Burford's historic buildings. This Elizabethan house, rebuilt in the early 1800s, still has its Tudor gables and the heraldic arms over the doorway recall William Lenthall (1591–1662) who lived here and was elected Speaker to the Long Parliament in 1640.

the walk

1 Walk out of the car park and turn right along **Church Lane**, passing the church to reach High Street. Turn right to the River Windrush, cross it and go right again at a mini-roundabout towards Fulbrook. Keep going for 0.75 mile (1.2km), passing in slow succession the Carpenters Arms, a turning to Swinbrook and the Masons Arms. Then, beyond Upper End, on the left, look for a **waymarked footpath** leaving on the right.

3h00 — **6.75 MILES** — **10.9 KM** — **LEVEL 123**

MAP: OS Explorer OL45 The Cotswolds

START/FINISH: Burford: Large car park to east of Windrush, near parish church; grid ref: SP 253122

PATHS: field and riverside paths, tracks, country roads, 7 stiles

LANDSCAPE: undulating Windrush Valley to the east of Burford

PUBLIC TOILETS: Burford High Street

TOURIST INFORMATION: Burford, tel 01993 823558

THE PUB: The Swan, Swinbrook

Getting to the start

Burford stands by a crossroads of the A40, between Oxford and Cheltenham, and the A361 north from Swindon. The car park, from which the walk begins, is signed along Church Lane from the A361 in the town centre.

Researched and written by:
Nick Channer, Dennis Kelsall

2 Climb beyond a dip to the field edge and swing right. Follow the boundary for 250yds (229m) to a waymark and bear left across the field, rising along an obvious fold in the hillside. Walk through a gap in the hedge on the far side and cross the subsequent field to an opening in the hedgerow. Keep going in the next field towards a curtain of **woodland**, there meeting a track.

3 Follow it to the right through the trees, breaking cover to join with another track from the left. Walk between fields for 0.5 mile (800m), passing a row of cottages and then **Paynes Farm**. Just after the farm, turn right onto a waymarked track and climb to a gate. Continue on an unfenced field track towards trees, descending beyond them to a gate. Carry on between hedges up the hill to a lane.

4 Turn right and walk down into a dip, where a sign for Widford directs you left across a stone stile. Follow a grassy ride through verdant **Dean Bottom**, later crossing another stile, to pass **Widford's St Oswald's Church**. You will find the entrance around to the right.

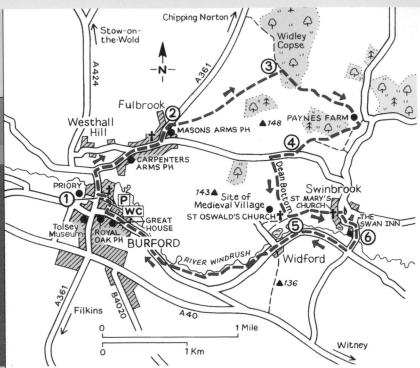

5 The onward route, however, lies to the
left, swinging away just before a
cottage ahead. Follow a faint field track to a
stile beside a gate. Keep going across
another stile, finally leaving through a gate
in the far wall. A walled path then leads you
to **St Mary's Church** at Swinbrook. Walk out
onto a lane and turn right to The Swan inn.

6 Carry on across the River Windrush,
soon reaching a crossroads by the
village **cricket green**. Walk right to **Widford**.
Some 250yds (229m) after a junction in the
hamlet, leave at a waymark on the right.
Follow a riverside path across a series of
stiles, eventually rejoining the lane. Go
right towards Burford, shortly passing the
Great House to reach the Royal Oak. There,
turn right into Guildenford and return to the
car park.

*Burford: a medieval bridge with the slender
church spire behind*

The Swan

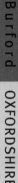

WALK

Burford

OXFORDSHIRE

The setting of this 400-year-old former mill cannot fail to impress. Rambling and creeper-clad, this unspoilt country inn sits beside a pretty bridge over the crystal clear River Windrush in a peaceful valley and village. Full of charm and character it retains some of its original features, with flagstone floors in the classic tap room and ancient oak beams and open fires in the hop-adorned main bar and cosy dining room. Old settles, a log-burning stove, traditional pub games, a good range of ales and decent farm ciders can also be found in the comfortable taproom. No piped music, no intrusive electronic games – a country pub to really relax in and savour. On sunny days head for the pretty walled side garden or enjoy a pint at a bench out by the lane and river.

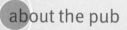

about the pub

The Swan
Swinbrook, Burford
Oxfordshire OX18 4DY
Tel: 01993 822165

DIRECTIONS: village signposted off the A40 east of Burford; pub is located by the bridge over the River Windrush

PARKING: 10

OPEN: daily

FOOD: no food Sunday evening

BREWERY/COMPANY: free house

REAL ALE: Wadworth 6X, Greene King IPA & Old Speckled Hen, Archers Village

DOGS: allowed in the bar on leads

Food

Choose smoked salmon and cucumber baguette, cottage pie, spaghetti bolognaise or steak and kidney pie from the lunchtime menu. Evening dishes take in fillet steak, seafood risotto, chicken with mango and mint sauce, and daily fish specials.

Family facilities

Well-behaved children are welcome inside away from the bar and smaller portions of the main menu dishes are available.

Alternative refreshment stops

Burford has plenty of places to eat and drink – from hotel restaurants to pub dining rooms and tea shops.

☛ Where to go from here

Visit the nearby village of Filkins, home to the Swinford Museum which illustrates west Oxfordshire's rural heritage. The village boasts a Victorian church built in the French Gothic style and was once the home of Sir Stafford Cripps, chancellor of the exchequer (1947–50) in the post-war Labour cabinet. At Minster Lovell you can visit the ruins of the 15th-century Minster Lovell Hall and see a medieval dovecote.

Buscot to Kelmscott

On the Thames Path to the home of William Morris.

Champion of Fine Craftsmanship

The village of Kelmscott is famous for its connections with William Morris (1834–96), founder of the Arts and Crafts Movement. Today he is best remembered for his furnishing designs, rich with flowers, leaves and birds.

Throughout his life Morris dedicated himself to a movement against what he saw as the vulgar tastes of his day, with its sentimentality, clutter and gaudy gewgaws. He put a new value on craftsmanship,

studying and experimenting with the techniques of ages past, and developing a style of apparent simplicity combined with functionality. He took it upon himself to educate too, with pronouncements such as 'Have nothing in your houses that you do not know to be useful, or believe to be beautiful' emphasising the place of good design in everyday life. His philosophy of design became hugely influential and Morris looked to medieval artists and architects for his inspiration.

Kelmscott Manor itself dates from 1570 and became Morris's country home in 1871. It's a mellow old place, built of the local

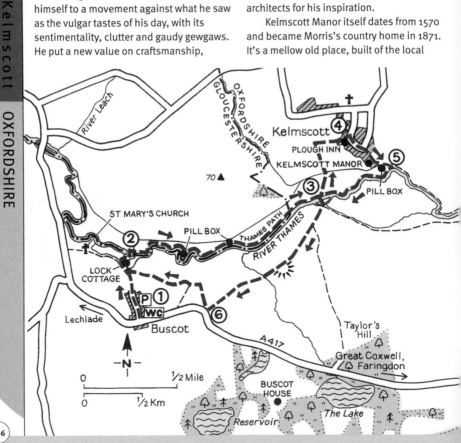

A quiet lane beside the Thames, heading towards Kelmscott

1h45 · **4.5 MILES** · **7.2 KM** · **LEVEL 123**

grey limestone, with mullioned windows and high pointed gables topped by ball finials. Morris loved the manor for its integrity and austerity, and for the harmony of the house in its setting. Now owned by the Society of Antiquaries of London, the house is open to the public on Wednesdays and some Saturdays through the summer.

As a memorial to the great man, several structures were designed to his principles and built in Kelmscott village, notably Memorial Cottages and next-door Manor Cottages. Reflecting traditional style but with a modern, practical twist, they blend effortlessly into the village and were overseen by his widow Jane and daughter May. On a wider scale, Morris's work did much for the emergence of a Cotswold identity in the 1920s. Morris is buried with his wife and daughters in the churchyard at Kelmscott, under a modest tombstone, its only adornment the elegant lettering designed by Philip Webb.

the walk

1 Before beginning the walk proper, stroll back from the car park to admire **Buscot's arcaded pump**. Retrace your steps and continue along the lane, signed to the weir. Bear right where it forks beside the village field, go across a bridge and then immediately turn right on a footpath past **Lock Cottage**. Follow the path over the weir and cross the lock gate.

2 Go right, over a stile and skirt the field edge to another bridge below the main weir. Turn right and follow the **Thames Path**

MAP: OS Explorer 170 Abingdon, Wantage & Vale of White Horse

START/FINISH: National Trust car park (free) in Buscot, signed 'Buscot Weir'; grid ref: SU 231976

PATHS: riverside paths, fields, village lanes, 5 stiles

LANDSCAPE: open, flat lands of the Thames floodplain

PUBLIC TOILETS: at the start

TOURIST INFORMATION: Witney, tel 01993 775802

THE PUB: The Plough Inn, Kelmscott

❶ An easy, level walk suitable for all ages; care to be taken with children on the riverside path.

Getting to the start

The tiny hamlet of Buscot stands beside the A417, 2 miles (3.2km) south east of Lechlade on Thames. Turn off onto a lane to Buscot Locks, beside which you will find a tea room, toilets and a car park.

Researched and written by:
Dennis Kelsall, Ann F Stonehouse

Kelmscott OXFORDSHIRE

from field to field downstream beside the meandering river for 1.25 miles (2km), passing a couple of **wartime pill boxes** along the way. The roofs of Kelmscott eventually appear before you and then, entering trees, you will reach a bridge.

3 Walk past it to go through a gate just beyond and turn left up the field edge. At the far side cross a stile and two footbridges, then dog-leg left and right to continue at the edge of the next field with the hedge on your right. At the top, turn right along a sometimes overgrown path, which emerges onto a lane beside **The Plough Inn** at Kelmscott.

4 Go right in front of the pub and then bear left, following the lane past **Memorial Cottages** and **Manor Cottages**. Keep right to reach **Kelmscott Manor** and carry on along a track, passing another World War Two pill box before you come to the Thames.

what to look for

Look out for the charming relief carving of William Morris, set in the wall of the pair of Memorial Cottages at first floor height, between the windows. The great man is shown sitting under a tree, listening to the birds, with the old wool barn and summer house of the manor in the background.

Kelmscott Manor

5 Just before the river, turn right, cross a bridge and go through a gate to join the **Thames Path** once more. Over a stile, continue upriver through a gate, passing yet another pill box on your left. Go back through the gate by the footbridge, but now cross the river to a small **marina**. Bear left and right over a second bridge, climbing a stile to follow a track away. At the first bend, cross a ditch and then immediately leave the track, heading diagonally right across a field. At the corner cross a stile and footbridge by a fingerpost and turn right. Where the hedge then breaks, curve left to remain in the same field and climb along a track beside the continuing hedge, where there is a glimpse of **Buscot House** over to the left. Follow the track downhill and, as it then bends right, turn left over a footbridge. Continue on a path diagonally right across the next two fields.

6 Emerge through a gate by the main **A417** road, there turning right along an adjacent track. After 300yds (274m), look out for a **yellow waymark** and turn left through a gate. Over a stile veer left along the edge of the field, crossing another stile and a footbridge at the far end onto the village field. Return to the lane and retrace your steps to Buscot.

The Plough Inn

Built in 1631, the rambling Plough is situated along the dead-end village lane in sleepy Kelmscott, just a short stroll from the River Thames and Kelmscott Manor, once home to the artist and designer William Morris. Long a popular refreshment stop among the walking and boating fraternity, the pub has been sympathetically restored and refurbished inside, a new stylish and contemporary look mixing well with original flagstones, stone walls and the exposed beams and timbers of the 17th-century fabric of the building. Modern pub food is freshly prepared on the premises using local produce where possible. A peaceful overnight's rest is assured in well-equipped en suite bedrooms. Lovely garden and terrace for summer drinking.

about the pub

The Plough Inn
Kelmscott, Lechlade
Oxfordshire GL7 3HG
Tel: 01367 253543
www.theploughatkelmscott.co.uk

DIRECTIONS: village signposted off the A416 1 mile (1.6km) east of Lechlade. Pub in the village centre near Kelmscott Manor

PARKING: roadside parking or use village car park

OPEN: daily; closed Monday in winter

FOOD: daily

BREWERY/COMPANY: free house

REAL ALE: Hook Norton Bitter, Timothy Taylor Landlord, guest beer

DOGS: welcome in the bar

ROOMS: 8 en suite

Food

Beyond the extensive sandwich menu including pork and leek sausages with roast onion, local ham ploughman's and beef stir-fry with noodles on the bar menu, look out for slow-roasted belly pork with black pudding and apple mash and wide-ranging fish choices on the imaginative carte.

Family facilities

Children are welcome inside and there's a children's menu available as well as smaller portions of adult dishes. High chairs are also provided.

Alternative refreshment stops

Buscot Village Shop (closed Mondays) doubles as a tea room, also serving light lunches.

☞ Where to go from here

Make time to visit Kelmscott Manor (www.kelmscottmanor.co.uk), the country home of William Morris. Nearby is Buscot House, an 18th-century Adam-style house with a landscaped park, a splendid walled garden, and an extensive water garden designed by Harold Peto (www.nationaltrust.org.uk).

Kelmscott OXFORDSHIRE

Beyond Chipping Norton

From Chipping Norton to an ancient site associated with a charming legend.

Rollright Stones

Commanding a splendid position overlooking the rolling hills and valleys of the north east Cotswolds, the Rollright Stones comprise the Whispering Knights, the King's Men and the King Stone. These intriguing stones are steeped in myth and legend.

In reality the Rollright Stones form a group of prehistoric megalithic monuments created from large natural boulders found within about 600yds (549m) of the site. The stones are naturally pitted, giving them astonishing and highly unusual shapes. The Whispering Knights, of which there are five, are the remains of a Portal Dolmen burial chamber, probably constructed around 3800–3000 BC, long before the stone circle. It would have been very imposing in its day and it is the easternmost burial chamber of this kind in Britain. The King Stone stands alone and apart from the others, just across the county boundary in Warwickshire. The 8ft (2.4m) tall single standing stone was almost certainly erected to mark the site of a Bronze Age cemetery which was in use around 1800–1500 BC.

Finally you come to the King's Men Stone Circle – a ceremonial monument thought to have been built around 2500–2000 BC. There are more than 70 stones here but it has been said they are impossible to count.

No-one knows why this particular site was chosen to erect the stones. The origin of the stones remains a mystery. It is appropriate that the remote hilltop setting of these timeless stones has more than a hint of the supernatural about it.

the walk

1 Walk from the car park to the main A44 road and follow it downhill. Pass **Penhurst School** then veer right through a kissing gate. Skirt the left-hand edge of a recreation ground, aiming for another kissing gate. Descend to a bridge and, when the path forks, keep right. Go up the slope and stay straight ahead over successive stiles, crossing a drive and shortly arriving at a second one. Walk forward along the right-hand edge of the field opposite, continuing in the next field to a pair of gates in the bottom corner.

2 Emerging onto a track, follow it left for 0.75 mile (1.2km) towards **Salford**. Carry on into the village to a crossing of lanes, there turning right onto a track marked 'Trout Lakes' and '**Rectory Farm**'.

3 Follow the track for 0.5 mile (800m) to a right-hand bend. Go straight ahead through a gate, following the field edge to another gate and turn right in the next field. About 100yds (91m) before the field corner,

The 17th century church of St Philip, set in the lush green of the Oxfordshire countryside

strike left across the field to an opening in the boundary. Veer left, then immediately right to skirt the field. Cross a little stream and maintain your direction in the next field to reach a road.

4 Turn left up the hill, and after 0.5 mile (800m) go left again for Little Rollright, keeping right at a fork to wind round to **St Philip's Church**. After seeing the church, retrace your steps to the edge of the hamlet and take the **D'Arcy Dalton Way**, signed off on the left. Follow the path straight up the field to the road. Cross over and continue on the D'Arcy Dalton Way, maintaining your direction across an open field to a stile beneath some trees at the far side. However, do not cross, instead turn left up the field edge, soon passing the **Whispering Knights**.

5 On reaching the road, go left, but be careful as traffic moves quickly. You will find the **King Stone** and the **King's Men** on either side, some 200yds (183m) along. There is a small charge to look around them. Return past the Whispering Knights to the stile, this time crossing it and an immediate second stile to walk ahead on a grassy swathe. Emerging over a stile onto a track, turn right towards **Brighthill Farm**, passing beside the buildings to a stile at the end. Head diagonally right down the field to the corner and, crossing consecutive stiles into the next field, keep going with the boundary on your right. After encountering another stile and then a gate, bear away from the hedge, leaving the far side of the field onto a lane. Go left.

MAP: OS Explorer 191 Banbury, Bicester & Chipping Norton

START/FINISH: Chipping Norton: free car park off A44, in town centre; grid ref: SP 312269

PATHS: field paths and tracks, country roads, 10 stiles

LANDSCAPE: rolling hills on the Oxfordshire/Warwickshire border

PUBLIC TOILETS: at car park

TOURIST INFORMATION: Chipping Norton, tel 01608 644379

THE PUB: The Chequers, Chipping Norton

ℹ Although this is a long walk there are no overly steep climbs. Suitable for fitter, older family groups.

Getting to the start

Chipping Norton stands 12 miles (19.3km) south west of Banbury by the junction of the A361 and A44. The walk begins from a long-stay car park signed left off the A44 as it leaves the town centre for Moreton-in Marsh, opposite the entrance to the Somerfield supermarket car park.

Researched and written by:
Nick Channer, Dennis Kelsall

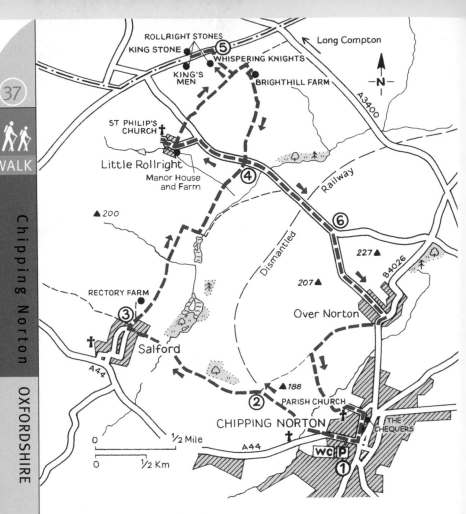

6 Keep right when you reach a fork and head towards **Over Norton**. Walk through the village to a T-junction and turn right. When the road shortly swings left by **Cleeves Corner**, keep ahead on a tarmac track signposted to Salford. After 0.5 mile (800m), when the hedges give way, look for a waymark on the left. Follow a path down the slope with the hedge on your right, continuing through two kissing gates and then alongside a stone wall to the parish church. Join Church Lane, which leads to a T-junction. Turn right and return to the town centre, passing **The Chequers** on the way. The car park lies to the right off the A44.

what to look for

The manor house at Little Rollright was once important. It was the home of William Blower who gave St Philip's Church its pinnacled tower in 1617. The church, which dates mostly from the 15th century, has two 17th-century monuments to the local Dixon and Blower families.

The Chequers

Standing next door to this bustling town's renowned theatre, The Chequers was built in the 16th century to provide lodgings for the stonemasons building St Mary's Church. An ale house ever since, it has a traditional look, with winter log fires, low ceilings, soft lighting and rug-strewn flagstone floors in the main bar, while the bright and airy conservatory-style restaurant has been created from the glassed over rear courtyard. A rural outpost for Fuller's Brewery, you'll find excellent beer, a global list of wine, a wide-ranging menu listing freshly prepared food, and a friendly welcome.

Food
For lunch tuck into honey-roast ham ploughman's, bacon and Brie sandwiches, or order beer battered cod and chips, spinach and mushroom lasagne, and specials like braised lamb shank with rosemary and redcurrant sauce. Evening additions may include roast cod fillet, duck breast and chargrilled steaks.

Family facilities
There are no special facilities but children are allowed in the bars, if eating, until 8pm; smaller portions of adult dishes are available.

Alternative refreshment stops
Chipping Norton offers a variety of pubs, hotels and tea rooms. The rambling old Blue Boar has views of the Market Place and the town's many historic buildings. The Black Horse at Salford offers the chance to stop off for refreshment during the walk.

about the pub

The Chequers
Goddards Lane, Chipping Norton
Oxfordshire OX7 5NP
Tel: 01608 644717
www.chequers-pub.co.uk

DIRECTIONS: town centre, next to the theatre
PARKING: use town centre car parks
OPEN: daily; all day
FOOD: no food Sunday evening
BREWERY/COMPANY: Fuller's Brewery
REAL ALE: Fuller's Chiswick, London Pride, ESB & seasonal ales
DOGS: well-behaved dogs are welcome in the public bar

☛ **Where to go from here**
Visit Woodstock and Blenheim Palace (www.blenheimpalace.com), the home of the 11th Duke of Marlborough and birthplace of Winston Churchill. See the magnificent state rooms, fine furniture, paintings and tapestries, view the sweeping lawns and stroll through the landscaped grounds.

Around Hook Norton

Meander through the rolling countryside surrounding the famous Hook Norton Brewery.

A Pint of Hooky

The Hook Norton Brewery is special in more ways than one. Locally brewed beers were once commonplace, but sadly not today, and neither will you see many six-storey Victorian tower breweries around, and the one at Hook Norton is the finest of its type. In fact, its equipment is still powered by a 25-horse-power steam engine, installed in 1899 when the brewery was extended to its present size. Buildings and machinery are not the only things to have remained constant throughout the years. The brewery was founded in 1849 by John Harris, and his great grandson and his son now manage the company between them. Quality beers ensured the firm's initial success, and the traditional methods of brewing employed then are still applied today. Hook Norton claims to be one of the few, if not the only brewery, never to have kegged its beers. Whilst a portion of the brew is bottled, the rest is cask conditioned, and within the vicinity of the brewery, is still delivered by horse-drawn dray. During the week there are guided tours around the brewery, which explain the process of brewing from start to finish, and afterwards there is an opportunity to sample a selection of the beers. You can

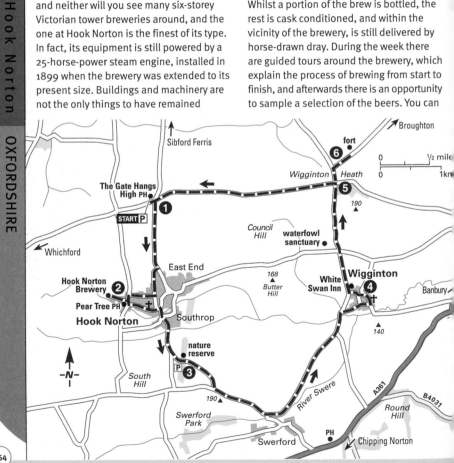

Hook Norton Brewery

2h30 **9.75 MILES** **15.7 KM** **LEVEL 123**

MAP: OS Explorer 191 Banbury, Bicester & Chipping Norton

START/FINISH: park at The Gate Hangs High, 1 mile (1.6km) north of Hook Norton, but please ask first; grid ref: SP 354349

TRAILS/TRACKS: country roads and lanes

LANDSCAPE: hilly countryside surrounding the village of Hook Norton

PUBLIC TOILETS: none on route

TOURIST INFORMATION: Chipping Norton, tel 01608 644379

CYCLE HIRE: none locally

THE PUB: The Gate Hangs High, Hook Norton

🔴 Care along minor roads, particularly on the return to The Gate Hangs High where traffic can move fast

Getting to the start

Hook Norton is 5 miles (8km) north east of Chipping Norton, a little way north of the A361 to Banbury. The ride is described from The Gate Hangs High, a fine country pub beside a crossroads 1 mile (1.6km) north of the village along the lane to Sibford Ferris.

Why do this cycle ride?

This is an excuse to visit the Hook Norton Brewery, but having said that, the countryside around the village is deserving of exploration. The route is hilly, and at its high point leads to an Iron Age fort, which in its day must have held a commanding position over the surrounding countryside.

Researched and written by: Dennis Kelsall

also wander around a fascinating museum, packed with memorabilia from Hook Norton's last 150 years.

the ride

1 Leave the pub car park and go left to the adjacent junction, there turning right to enjoy a gentle free-wheeling descent into **Hook Norton**. Approaching the edge of the village, swing right into Bourne Lane, and then at the fire station, go right again into The Bourne. When you reach the end, follow the lane down to the **Pear Tree Inn**, leaving immediately before it along Brewery Lane on the right. You will find the **Hook Norton Brewery**, museum and visitor centre at the end.

2 Return to the Pear Tree Inn and go right and then immediately left, cycling through the older part of the village to reach the church. Carry on a little further to a junction opposite the village shop, there dropping right, following a sign to **Swerford**. Keep with the main lane as it falls to a brook, briefly rising over Brick Hill before dipping across a second stream. The way now climbs ahead out of the village along Swerford Road, shortly curving left in front of a junction to a bridge spanning Hook Norton Cutting; the course of a disused railway and now a small **nature reserve**.

3 Carry on up the hill, joining another lane from the right at the top, to drop beyond into **Swerford**. The gradient steepens towards the bottom, where at a sharp bend you should turn off left onto a narrow lane that gently rises along the valley. Reaching a T-junction after a mile (1.6km), go left down the hill towards **Wiggington**, bearing right where the road splits at the bottom. Climbing into the village, swing right, skirting the perimeter of the enclosed raised green. Take the first on the left to pass in front of the church.

4 Wind left past the Old Rectory and then go right at the next two junctions, climbing away beyond the **Old White Swan Inn**. At a crossroads not far beyond, keep ahead, resuming your ascent past a **waterfowl sanctuary** and children's animal centre. Before long the gradient begins to

ease, leading you on to another crossroads on the edge of Wiggington Heath.

5 Go straight over, and stay with the main lane where it shortly bends to the right. Continue for a further 0.25 mile (400m) before stopping to have a look at an **Iron Age fort**; the road actually cuts straight through it. The area to the right is incorporated within a golf course, however, the earthworks on the other side remain impressively prominent, clearly defining the defensive line of the enclosure, and a bridleway running beside it offers the opportunity for a closer look.

6 Return to the crossroads and turn right, signed to Hook Norton. Your earlier uphill work is now rewarded, for the road undulates gently downwards for the next 2 miles (3.2km), taking you back to **The Gate Hangs High**. Go carefully along the road, since traffic often moves quickly along this straight stretch of road.

Beer is transported the traditional way

The Gate Hangs High

Originally a toll house, this charming country pub stands at an isolated rural crossroads and is well worth tracking down. Its name refers to the toll gate which was hung high so that chickens and ducks could go under but large animals had to stop. As the pub sign indicates – 'the Gate hangs high and hinders none, Refresh and pay, and travel on' – everyone is welcome at the pub. A traditional atmosphere fills the long, low-ceilinged bar with its assorted furnishings, hop-adorned bar counter, and a huge inglenook fireplace with gleaming copper hood. The pub is handy for the Rollright Stones and it's just down the lane from the famous Hook Norton Brewery from where the pub sources its tip-top ales.

Food

Changing menus may take in smoked salmon pasta, sausages and mash with onion gravy, salmon and prawn pie and rib-eye steak with pepper and brandy. Good value mid-week set menu and Sunday roast lunches (booking advisable).

Family facilities

Children of all ages are welcome in the pub. Expect a children's menu, smaller portions of adult meals and high chairs for younger family members. Excellent seating in the rear garden with lovely rural views.

Alternative refreshment stops

In Hook Norton village you will find the Pear Tree Inn and the Sun Inn (also owned by Hook Norton Brewery), and you will pass the Old White Swan at Wigginton on the route.

☞ Where to go from here

Take a tour of the Hook Norton Brewery (www.hook-norton-brewery.co.uk) and learn more about the art of brewing beer. Visit Broughton Castle, an early 14th- and mid-16th-century house with moat and gatehouse, or head back to Wigginton as the children will love to see the Wildfowl Sanctuary and Children's Farm.

about the pub

The Gate Hangs High
Hook Norton, Banbury
Oxfordshire OX15 5DF
Tel: 01608 737870
www.gatehangshigh.com

DIRECTIONS: see Getting to the start
PARKING: 40
OPEN: daily; all day Sunday
FOOD: daily; all day Sunday
BREWERY/COMPANY: Hook Norton Brewery
REAL ALE: Hook Norton Bitter, Old Hooky & seasonal ales
ROOMS: 4 en suite

The villages of Great Tew and Little Tew

Take a stroll through one of Oxfordshire's loveliest villages before exploring undulating countryside to the south.

The fall and rise of Great Tew

Arthur Mee, in his book *The King's England – Oxfordshire*, says that 'if our England is a garden, Great Tew is one of its rare plots.' Most would agree. The village is a gem of a place.

Designed as an estate village in the 19th century, with the intention of blending architectural beauty with utility and management, Great Tew went into decline in later years and virtually became derelict. However, the village has been given a new lease of life, with many of the thatched and ironstone cottages carefully restored, and it is now a designated Conservation Area.

The origin of its name is unclear, but Tew is thought to mean 'ridge', of which there are a great many in the area. The village has a long history and in later years became closely associated with Lucius Carey, 2nd Viscount Falkland, Secretary of State to Charles I. A later owner, G F Stratton, who inherited Great Tew in 1800, resided in a rather modest late 17th- or early 18th-century house which stood at the southern end of the village. During the early years of the 19th century, Stratton engaged in an ill-fated trial in estate management.

The estate changed hands several times before being acquired by Matthew Robinson Boulton. Outlying farms were rebuilt, cottages were re-thatched and other features such as mullioned windows and stone door heads were added. The estate

remained the home of the Boulton family for many years. Between 1914 and 1962 Great Tew was administered by trustees but by now the local workforce had decreased and the estate was all but abandoned.

It was Major Eustace Robb, an old Etonian and descendant of the Boulton family, who moved to the village with the aim of halting its steady decline. His efforts certainly paid off. A stroll through the village today is marked by a conspicuous air of affluence.

the walk

1 From the car park at the edge of Great Tew, walk left along the main lane and go past the turning into the village. Immediately beyond the junction, leave through a gate on the right, the path signposted to Little Tew. Climb diagonally across the field, heading for **Court Farm** on the brow of the hill. Enter the farmyard over a stile by a gate and bear right, skirting

Above: Little Tew is on the route of the walk

1h45 · **3.75 MILES** · **6 KM** · **LEVEL 1 2 3**

MAP: OS Explorer 191 Banbury, Bicester & Chipping Norton

START/FINISH: Free car park in Great Tew; grid ref: SP 395293

PATHS: field paths and tracks, stretches of quiet road, 3 stiles

LANDSCAPE: rolling parkland and farmland on edge of Cotswolds

PUBLIC TOILETS: none on route

TOURIST INFORMATION: Chipping Norton, tel 01608 644379

THE PUB: The Falkland Arms, Great Tew

❗ Paths at the edge of some crop fields may become overgrown in summer and may be difficult for young children

Getting to the start

Great Tew stands alongside the B4022, just south of its junction with the A361 and 7 miles (11.3km) south west of Banbury. There is a small car park on the edge of the village beside the lane as it enters from the north.

Researched and written by:
Nick Channer, Dennis Kelsall

---

some silos to find another gate and stile behind them. Follow the right-hand field boundary to the top corner, emerging over a final stile at a junction.

2 Cross to a path at the left angle of the junction, again signposted to Little Tew. Head diagonally across the field, passing to the right of a **transmitter**. On reaching a lane, turn right and walk down the hill into **Little Tew**. At a junction by the church of St John the Evangelist turn left towards Enstone.

3 The lane climbs out of the village over a rise, dropping on the far side to a **bridge** bounded by white railings. Just beyond, go through an opening in the left-hand hedge into a field and follow the left boundary away. Through a gate in the corner, continue ahead in a meadow, shortly joining a track from a house, over to the left. Follow it out to the road.

WALK

4 Be careful, for traffic moves quickly, as you cross to a track opposite, signed to Sandford. It eventually swings left over a bridge in front of **Tracey Barn Farm**. Immediately turn right and walk away at the field edge. Entering trees at the far side, a track leads on through a gate, but leave it after 50yds (46m) through a small waymarked gate on the left. Climb away at the edge of successive fields. Approaching a **lodge** at the top, leave the field through a gate and walk along its drive out to the road by a junction.

5 Cross to the lane opposite, signposted for Great Tew, and follow it down past the entrance to **St Michael's Church**, which lies peacefully amid the trees of the parkland

what to look for

Little Tew is worth close inspection. The church, built by George Street, dates back to 1835 and the Methodist chapel to 1871. The Grange, also by Street, was built as a vicarage about the same time as the church. The school and almshouses were constructed in the 1860s. Walk along the splendid avenue of laurels and traveller's joy leading to Great Tew's fine medieval church, which lies peacefully amid the trees of the parkland. The church walk was originally the carriage drive to the mansion of Lucius Carey, 2nd Viscount Falkland.

on the right. Carry on, passing the school to return to the **village green**, at the back of which, you will find The Falkland Arms.

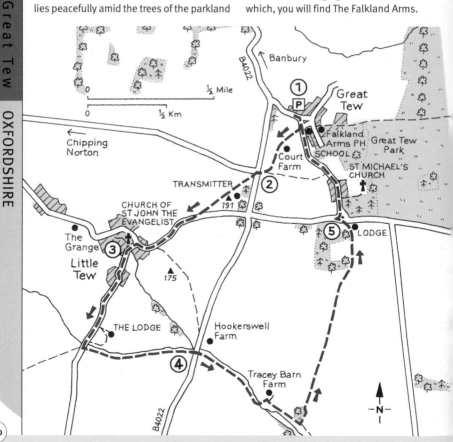

The Falkland Arms

An unspoiled and historic village is the tranquil setting for this 500-year-old, creeper-clad, Cotswold-stone inn which takes its name from Lucius Carey, 2nd Viscount Falkland, who inherited the manor of Great Tew in 1629. Nestling at the end of a charming row of Cotswold-stone cottages – the quintessential English village scene – The Falkland Arms is a classic gem. The intimate bar features flagstone floors, high-backed settles, a huge inglenook fireplace with winter log fire, and a collection of jugs and mugs hangs from the old beams. A pretty garden is shaded by a large hornbeam tree, complete with dovecote.

Food

Home-made specials such as beef and ale pie or salmon and broccoli fishcakes supplement the basic lunchtime menu (baguettes & ploughman's), served in the bar or the pub garden. In the evening, booking is essential for dinner in the small, non-smoking dining room. Expect parsnip soup or grilled goat's cheese salad, followed by chicken breast with bacon and mushrooms in shallot sauce, or salmon and prawns with lemon and dill sauce.

Family facilities

Children are welcome in the separate dining area at lunchtimes only.

Alternative refreshment stops

Nearby Chipping Norton has a range of restaurants, pubs and cafés.

☛ Where to go from here

At North Leigh, near Woodstock, is the remains of a large and well-built Roman courtyard villa. In Woodstock you can visit the award-winning Oxfordshire Museum and learn more about the archaeology, landscape and wildlife of the county.

about the pub

The Falkland Arms
Great Tew, Chipping Norton
Oxfordshire OX7 4DB
Tel: 01608 683653
www.falklandarms.org.uk

DIRECTIONS: see Getting to the start; pub along dead-end lane by the village stores, opposite the church

PARKING: use village hall car park

OPEN: daily; all day Saturday & Sunday mid-July–September

FOOD: daily; restaurant only in evening; no food Sunday evening

BREWERY/COMPANY: Wadworth Brewery

REAL ALE: Wadworth 6X & Henry's IPA, 4 guest beers

DOGS: allowed on a lead

ROOMS: 5 en suite

The Oxford waterway

Follow a quiet canal to meet the Thames in Britain's most famous university city.

Oxford Canal

The Oxford Canal took over 30 years to build, its 91 miles (146km) running up £307,000 by the time it finally opened in 1790. Begun by James Brindley, it took a sinuous contour-hugging route to minimise the locks and aqueducts required. But the economy was double-edged, for although construction costs were reduced, passage time increased, and to stave off competition in the 1820s, Brunel was asked to straighten some of the bends. Financed by a consortium that included Oxford University, the City Corporation and the Duke of Marlborough, the canal brought coal from pits at Hawkesbury near Coventry. It quickly became profitable and managed to survive the steam revolution of the 19th century, carrying materials for the construction of the Midland railways and then reducing its tolls to maintain its share of traffic. Decline, however, was inevitable and by the early 1950s commercial traffic had all but ceased.

Oxford's university is thought to date from Henry II's reign, set up to accommodate English students thrown out of Paris by Louis VII. It comprises 41 separate colleges, many of them founded by rich monastic houses and bishops; Magdalen College was established by a Bishop of Winchester in 1458 and Queens College in 1540 by the chaplain of Queen Philippa, Edward III's

wife. A tradition of museums stems from this great seat of learning, with collections on every possible theme. The Museum of History of Science has one of Einstein's blackboards – complete with equations – while the Ashmolean collection includes Guy Fawkes' lantern and Henry VIII's stirrups.

the ride

1 Turning right from the car park, pedal back through the village to reach a pair of consecutive **bridges**. Leave the road immediately over the first, dismounting to negotiate a flight of downward **steps** on the left to the tow path .

2 Oxford lies to the right, the way shortly bridged by the railway and then running tree-lined past house gardens on the far bank. The residential suburbs of Oxford spill onto the canal itself, and many boats are

A houseboat on the Oxford Canal

2h00 **9.5 MILES** **15.3 KM** **LEVEL 1**23

SHORTER ALTERNATIVE ROUTE

1h30 — **6 MILES** **9.5 KM** **LEVEL 1**23

permanently moored and serve as accommodation. Further on, wetland an marsh on the right, **Trap Grounds**, is managed as a **nature reserve**. Such mars areas were once common around the old where willows and osiers provided withi for basket-making. The reserve provides last local refuge for the elusive water rail where the timid bird finds secluded nest sites amongst the thick vegetation. Furth on, although the surroundings become increasingly urban, the corridor of the ca retains a pleasant isolation.

3 Before long, a **cast-iron bridge** appe ahead where there is a choice of pa Take the middle one crossing the bridge and continue on a narrow strip of land separating the canal from the **River Thames**. The path carries on for a little o 0.5 mile (800m) before reaching the car abrupt end at **Oxford**. Oxford's heart lie the left, and there is much to see in this distinguished ancient city. However, as some of the streets are very busy, you may prefer to secure your bike and wan around on foot. Return along the canal to **Wolvercote** after your visit.

4 Following the canal in the other direction from Wolvercote takes you away from the city, passing beneath a couple of starkly functional bridges supporting the main roads. The tow pat then crosses Duke's Cut, a short arm th connects to the River Thames. Keep ahe beside the main canal past **Duke's Lock** pedalling beyond a disused railway brid and another road bridge (where Nationa Cycle Route 5 leaves for Woodstock), lat reaching **Kidlington Green Lock**.

MAP: OS Explorer 180 Oxford

START/FINISH: car park in Wolvercote; grid ref: SP 487094

TRAILS/TRACKS: surfaced canal tow path , short road section

LANDSCAPE: canal through Oxford's fringes

PUBLIC TOILETS: at car park

TOURIST INFORMATION: Oxford, tel 01865 726871

CYCLE HIRE: Bee-Line, 61–63 Cowley Road, Oxford, tel 01865 246615

THE PUB: The Trout Inn, Lower Wolvercote

🛈 Steps down to tow path at start (unless you start at Thrupp); unguarded canal tow paths shared with pedestrians; low-arched bridges; busy roads in Oxford.

Getting to the start

The ride begins from Wolvercote, which lies just north of Oxford near the junction of the A40 and A44 roads. Follow a minor road from the roundabout through the village to find a car park at a bend on the left.

Why do this cycle ride?

Oxford is best approached by bike. This uncomplicated ride takes you along the canal from one of its quiet suburbs, where there is a splendid Morse pub on the very banks of the Thames, almost to its heart. For a rural ride, follow the canal in the other direction to the attractive canal-side hamlet of Thrupp.

Researched and written by: Dennis Kelsall

5 Another mile (1.6km) lies between you and **Roundham Lock** as the canal slowly climbs from the upper Thames valley towards Banbury and the Midlands. Later on a small **industrial area** unobtrusively stands away from the canal, beyond which is a handful of cottages. After passing beneath the A4260, the tow path briefly follows the main road to the **Jolly Boatman pub**.

6 The waterway then swings away beside the tiny hamlet of **Thrupp**, where there is another pub and, opposite it, a much-weathered ancient cross. At the top end of the street, the tow path switches banks and the canal makes an abrupt turn in front of a maintenance yard. You can, of course continue north along the canal, but the hard surface later deteriorates making passage difficult. The way back to Wolvercote retraces your outward route.

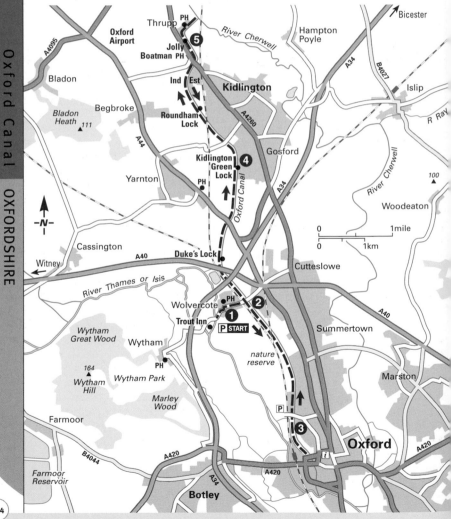

The Trout Inn

about the pub

The Trout Inn
Godstow Road, Lower Wolvercote
Oxford, Oxfordshire OX2 8PN
Tel: 01865 302071

DIRECTIONS: continue on from the car park to find the pub on the banks of the River Thames	
PARKING: 95	
OPEN: daily; all day	
FOOD: daily; all day	
BREWERY/COMPANY: Mitchells & Butler	
REAL ALE: Bass, guest beer	

Constructed in the 17th century from the ruins of Godstow Abbey, with a history that includes being torched by Parliamentarian troops, this famous medieval pub is serenely situated beside the River Thames and attracts thousands of visitors every year. In summer, the cobbled terrace beside the fast-running river with its weir makes a restful place for a quiet pint while watching the peacocks wandering round the terrace and catching a glimpse of the chub in the clear water. Inside, you'll find flagstones, beamed ceilings, bare boards and welcoming log fires throughout the several linked rooms, all adorned with hops, attractive pictures and country bric-a-brac. It has associations with Matthew Arnold, Lewis Carroll and Colin Dexter's Inspector Morse – numerous scenes from the TV series were filmed at the pub.

Food
A good choice of food offers baked whole trout with garlic mushrooms and cheddar mash, lemon chicken, beef, mushroom and Bass pie, or Cumberland sausage wrapped in Yorkshire pudding, with liver and bacon. Sandwiches and specials are listed on the blackboard.

Family facilities
Children are welcome in the pub if eating and there are smaller portions of some adult dishes. Supervised children will love the peacocks on the terrace and looking for the fish in the river.

Alternative refreshment stops
Choice of pubs in both Wolvercote and Oxford (and cafés) and two pubs beside the tow path at Thrupp.

☞ Where to go from here
Linger longer in Oxford, for there's plenty to see and do. In particular, some fascinating museums to visit: the Museum of Oxford (www.oxford.gov.uk/museum); the Ashmolean Museum of Art and Archaeology (www.ashmol.ox.ac.uk); the Pitt Rivers Museum (www.prm.os.ac.uk); the Oxford University Museum of Natural History (www.oum.ox.ac.uk); and the Museum of the History of Science (www.mhs.os.ac.uk). Why not visit the university and its various colleges (www.visitoxford.org) or take in the oldest botanic garden in the country with its collection of more than 8,000 species of plant (www.botanic-garden.ox.ac.uk)?

Acknowledgements

The Automobile Association would like to thank the following photographer and establishments for their assistance in the preparation of this book.

Photolibrary.com front cover b
Dennis Kelsall 19, 23, 25, 28, 31bl, 40, 45, 46, 47, 51, 52, 56, 59, 63tr, 63cl, 71, 75, 83, 87, 91, 95, 103, 107, 115, 119, 123, 127, 131, 139, 151, 155, 159, 163; Trout Inn, Lower Wolvercote 175; Wheatsheaf Inn, West End 111.

The remaining photographs are held in the Automobile Association's own Photo Library (AA World Travel Library) and were taken by the following photographers:

Adrian Baker 80; Peter Baker front cover cr, 33, 34, 35, 68/9; E A Bowness 12; Steve Day front cover cl, ccl, 4, 8/9, 29, 48/9, 49, 61, 84, 93, 100/1, 101, 105, 106, 108, 109, 120, 125, 126, 129, 132/3, 137, 149, 150, 152/3, 154, 160; Kenya Doran 69, 85, 94, 116/117, 118, 121, 172; Debbie Ireland 31tr, 41; Richard Ireland 24/5, 27, 38, 39, 43, 53, 55tl, 55tr, 58br, 64, 65, 67, 77t, 77b, 79, 96, 97, 99, 141, 142, 143tr, 143br, 147tr, 147cl, 167; Caroline Jones 62; Tom Mackie 15; S & O Mathews 58; Roy Rainford 157, 158; Tony Souter 14b, 112/3; Richard Surman 73, 89, 90; Wyn Voysey 13, 14t, 72, 135tr, 135b, 138, 145, 146, 165, 166, 168/9, 171; Harry Williams front cover ccr, 16, 17, 20/1.